Scott Basham

WORD 2007

D1502154

In easy steps is an imprint of Computer Step
Southfield Road · Southam
Warwickshire CV47 0FB · United Kingdom
www.ineasysteps.com

Notice of Liability
Every effort has been made to ensure that this book contains accurate
and current information. However, Computer Step and the author
shall not be liable for any loss or damage suffered by readers as a
result of any information contained herein.

Trademarks
Microsoft® and Windows® are registered trademarks of Microsoft
Corporation. All other trademarks are acknowledged as belonging to
their respective companies.

Printed and bound in the United Kingdom

ISBN-13 978-1-84078-319-3
ISBN-10 1-84078-319-2

Contents

7 The Page Layout Tab 121

8 The References Tab 129

9 The Mailings Tab 139

10 The Review Tab 147

11 The View Tab 161

12 Advanced Features 171

Index 187

1 Finding Your Way Around

This chapter quickly gets you started with Word 2007. It shows you how to launch Word and explains all the main areas in its screen layout. You will learn the basic controls and the way they are organized and accessed.

Introduction

Word processing was one of the first popular applications for the modern personal computer. In the early days it provided little more than the ability to enter and change text on the screen. As time went on, software and hardware improved so that features such as spell-checking and visual type effects became available. Over the years, the number of users increased dramatically.

Almost since the beginning, Microsoft Word has been acknowledged as a leader in its field. It is one of the best selling software applications in any category. It grew in complexity from a program with fewer than 50 menu commands to Word 2003 with over 250.

In creating Word 2007, Microsoft have completely redesigned its user interface. Gone are almost all of the menus and submenus of previous versions, to be replaced with visual controls that reconfigure themselves to suit what you are currently doing. Accordingly, this book works as a graphical teaching guide – wherever possible pictures and worked examples are used to demonstrate the concepts covered. It is not intended to replace Microsoft's documentation; instead you should view it as a way of getting up to speed quickly in a wide range of useful techniques.

The full range of Word's features is covered in this and the following chapters – from creating and editing simple text-based documents to tables, graphics, and publishing to the Web as well as more advanced techniques such as mail merging and structuring longer documents.

How to use this book

To gain maximum benefit from this book, make sure you are first familiar with the Windows operating environment (using the mouse, icons, menus, dialog boxes and so on). There are a number of books in the Easy Steps range that can help you here.

It is a good idea to start off by going through Chapters 1 and 2 fairly thoroughly, since these introduce basic concepts on which later examples depend. Once you've done this you can then freely dip into the other chapters as you like. There is a chapter for each of the Command Tabs in the new Word interface, so that this book is organized in the same way as Word itself.

Don't forget

It is always very important to experiment using your own examples – trying commands a few times on test documents will give you the fluency and confidence you will need when working for real.

Starting Word 2007

On some computers Word 2007 may have been installed with a desktop shortcut. If it has not been, here is how to start it up.

1 Click the Start button in the bottom left corner of the screen

2 If Microsoft Office Word 2007 appears in this menu then you can select it straight away

3 If it is not in the menu then click All Programs

4 The menu expands to show you a list of programs, and program groups represented with small folder icons

5 Click the folder labeled Microsoft Office to expand its list of programs

6 The list of Microsoft applications you see will depend on what has been installed on your PC

7 Click on the small icon for Microsoft Office Word 2007

Hot tip

These examples show the Windows Vista operating system. In earlier versions of Windows you can start Word by opening the Start menu and selecting All Programs, Microsoft Word.

9

Activation

When you first run Microsoft Word on your PC, you are prompted for a valid Product Key.

You can use Word up to 25 times without bothering to enter a Product Key. After this Word will work in Reduced Functionality Mode – this means you can only read documents; you cannot make any changes. Each time you start Word you are prompted to enter the Product Key; once this is done you can use all the features permitted by the license.

Activation is a process where Microsoft checks that the Product Key has not been used on more computers than are allowed by the software license.

When you enter your Product Key the Activation Wizard automatically runs. You can choose to run Activation later if you wish.

To Activate Microsoft Word

1 Click the Office Button in the top left of the screen, are then choose Word Options

2 Click the Resources button, and then Activate

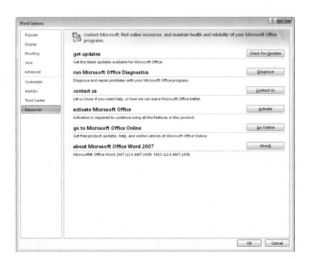

3 You will be given options to Activate over the Internet, or by using the telephone

---

Hot tip

In some cases Word will have been pre-installed on your PC, so the Product Key may already have been entered.

The Product Key is usually found printed on the outside of the install disc sleeve. Keep this in a safe place.

The Word 2007 Screen

Once Word is up and running, you should see the following screen – with all the elements illustrated here:

Office Button   Quick Access Toolbar   Command Tabs

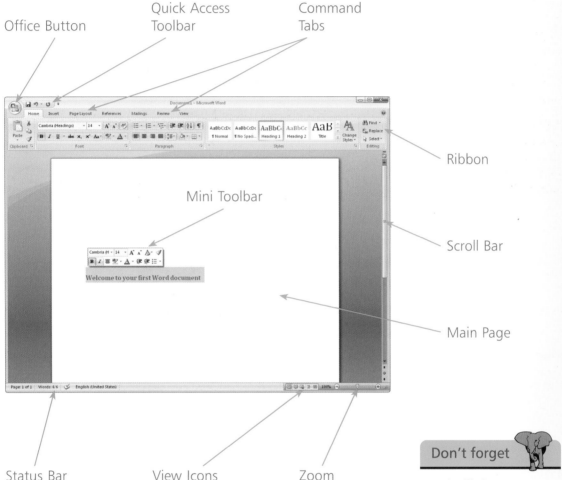

Mini Toolbar

Ribbon

Scroll Bar

Main Page

Status Bar   View Icons   Zoom

If you are familiar with previous versions of Word, you may be wondering what has happened to all the menus. Word 2007's interface has been completely redesigned to give you instant access to features relevant to the current task.

At first it may seem as if there is a lot to learn. Don't worry, though, as the Office Button, the Quick Access Toolbar, the Mini Toolbar and the Ribbon with its Command Tabs are all covered in the next few pages.

Don't forget

Word will show you different tools and palettes depending on your current activity – so do not worry if your screen does not match exactly with this illustration.

The Office Button

In the top left corner of the screen is the Office Button. It looks like this:

This gives you access to Word's main menu – from here you can create, open, close and print documents, and perform other activities besides.

Using the Office Button Menu

1 Click the Office Button in the top left of the screen to access the menu

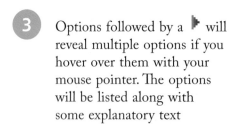

2 Options followed by three dots (...) will take you to a dialog box. For example, choosing Open... will show you a dialog asking you to choose which file to open

3 Options followed by a ► will reveal multiple options if you hover over them with your mouse pointer. The options will be listed along with some explanatory text

4 At the bottom right corner are additional buttons for accessing Word's global options, and for exiting Word altogether

5 You can also open the Office Button Menu using the keyboard. Hold down the Alt key and press F. If you keep holding the Alt key down you will see the keyboard shortcut for each option clearly marked

Don't forget

As with most Windows programs, you can use keyboard shortcuts for menu options. The underlined letter indicates which key to press – for example, the shortcut for the item labeled Open... is the letter "O".

The Ribbon

Near the top of the screen, the Ribbon gives you immediate access to a wide range of useful controls. These are organized in Tabs, only one of which is active at any time. In the example below the Home Tab is showing basic text editing and formatting features.

Hot tip

In this example the highlighted text changes its appearance as the controls in the Ribbon are used. It is currently formatted using the style "Subtitle". As the mouse hovers over the style "Title" the text temporarily changes its format to preview this style. For more about this new auto-preview feature in Word 2007 see Chapter 3: "Formatting Text".

Using different Tabs in the Ribbon

1 Click on the Insert Tab's title to activate it. You will see it is subdivided into eight sections

2 Double-click on the currently active Tab to hide the Ribbon temporarily. This is useful if you want to maximize the amount of screen space available for viewing and editing your document

3 A single click on any Tab heading will restore the Ribbon to its normal size

The Quick Access Toolbar

The Quick Access Toolbar is the small collection of tools at the top of the screen next to the Office Button.

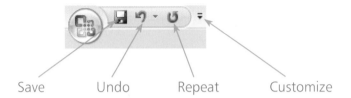

Save   Undo   Repeat   Customize

Customizing the Quick Access Toolbar

1 Click the Customize icon on the Quick Access Toolbar and select a command or choose More Commands... to see the full list

2 In the dialog that appears, select the "Choose commands from" value to see a list of Word commands

3 If you want your customizations to be global, make sure "For all documents" is selected under Customize Quick Access Toolbar

4 Add icons by double-clicking in the left-hand list, or click once to select and then choose Add>>

5 Remove icons by double-clicking in the right-hand list, or click once to select and then click on the Remove button

6 Click OK when done, or Cancel to abandon your changes

The Mini Toolbar

Whenever you have some text selected the Mini Toolbar will appear nearby. It gives you immediate access to the most commonly-used text formatting options.

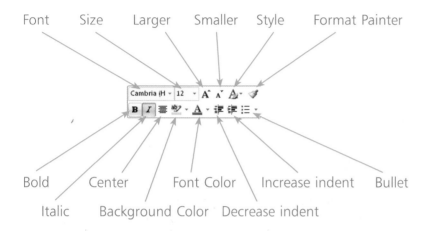

Font   Size   Larger   Smaller   Style   Format Painter

Bold   Center   Font Color   Increase indent   Bullet

Italic   Background Color   Decrease indent

Using the Mini Toolbar

1   Type some text and then select it by dragging across it with the mouse

2   Start with the mouse directly over the selected text, and then gradually move upwards. The Mini Toolbar will fade into view just above the text (see illustration below). As you move up towards the Mini Toolbar, it will become more solid

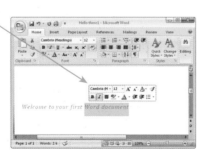

3   Click on one of the controls within the Mini Toolbar to change the appearance of your selected text

Hot tip

If the Mini Toolbar fails to appear when you hover over some text with your mouse, try right-clicking. A pop-up context menu will appear with the Mini Toolbar immediately above.

The Status Bar

The Status Bar is the horizontal strip at the bottom of the Word screen. It normally shows details of general settings and display options, and can be used for adjusting the zoom level.

Customizing the Status Bar

1 Right-click anywhere on the Status Bar to call up the Status Bar Configuration menu

2 All the Status Bar options are listed along with their current values. For example, in this illustration we can see that the Vertical Page Position is 3.9 inches – even though this is not normally displayed in the Status Bar

16

3 Click on a menu item to add it to or remove it from the Status Bar

4 Click anywhere other than the menu to close it when you have finished

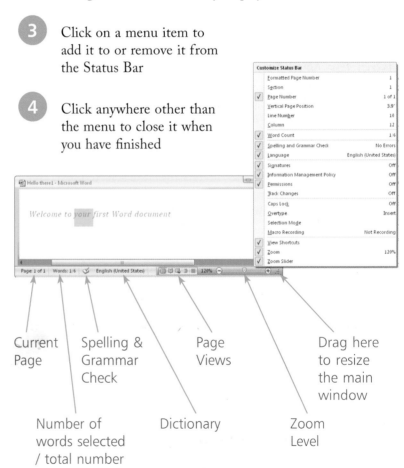

Current Page

Spelling & Grammar Check

Page Views

Drag here to resize the main window

Number of words selected / total number of words

Dictionary

Zoom Level

Command Tabs

The Home Tab
This gives you access to basic text editing and formatting options. It is illustrated at the top of page 13.

The Insert Tab
This allows you to add items such as graphics and tables.

Each of these Command Tabs has its own chapter later on in this book.

The Page Layout Tab
This lets you work with general layout options such as margins and columns, or apply a consistent Theme to a document.

The References Tab
References include Tables of Contents, Indexes, Citations, Bibliography, Captions and Tables of Authorities.

The Mailings Tab
This gives you access to Word's Mail Merge features.

The Review Tab
This allows you to track changes, as well as access proofing tools.

The View Tab
From here you can choose a view, and which elements to hide.

Contextual Tabs

Contextual Tabs appear only when necessary. This helps Word's screen display to be reasonably uncluttered as you only see the tools appropriate to your current activity.

For example, if you are editing a table you will see the Table Tools contextual tabs. These consist of a Tab for Design controls, and another for Layout.

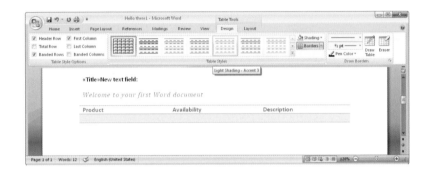

Don't forget

For more information on the Drawing Tools and Tables, see Chapter 6: "The Insert Tab".

Another example is the Drawing Tools – these appear if you have a graphic selected. Under the Drawing Tools heading is a Format Tab, which allows you to customize the appearance, size and positioning of your graphic items.

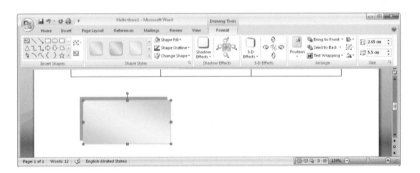

Sometimes you may see the same set of controls appear in several different Tabs. In the above example, the Insert Shapes tools are part of the Drawing Tools > Format tab. You may have noticed that you can also find these tools within the Insert Command Tab illustrated on the previous page.

Getting Help

1 Move your mouse over a command in the Ribbon

2 After a few moments a Super Tooltip appears, showing you the name of the command (useful if it is displayed only as an icon in the Ribbon). You will also see an explanation of its function

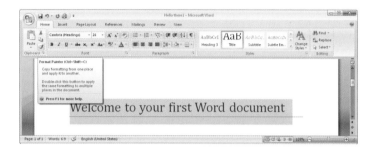

3 The ⬚ icon indicates that a dialog box will open if you click on it. If you just hover over it with the mouse, however, the Super Tooltip will include a preview image of the dialog – as in the example below

4 For more online information about any of Word's features, press the F1 key or click on the ⓦ icon in the top right corner of the screen

5 You will see an explanation of the control in question. If your mouse was not pointing at any controls when you pressed F1 then a general searchable Help window appears

Hot tip

If you have an active Internet connection, then you can also access Microsoft's online help content. If the indicator in the lower right corner of the Help window is set to Offline then click directly on it and select "Show content from Office Online".

Galleries

The ⯆ symbol indicates that a Gallery of items is available within a particular control. The Text Styles Gallery has an automatic preview feature, which allows you to see the effects of a Style before you decide to use it.

Using the Gallery of Text Styles

1 Select some text in your document

2 Make sure the Home Command Tab is active. If it is not then click on Home in the Ribbon

3 Click on the ⯆ icon in the lower right hand corner of the Styles controls. The Styles Gallery appears

Don't forget

For more help with basic text editing see the next chapter "The Home Tab" and Chapter 3: "Formatting Text".

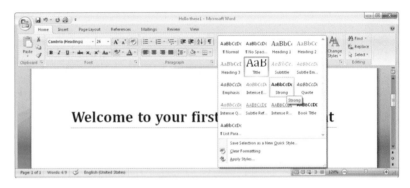

4 As you hover over a Style, your text changes to preview its effect

5 If you want to apply the Style permanently to the text then click on it. Alternatively, if you do not want to apply the new Style then just move the mouse elsewhere

6 When you have finished, click anywhere in the Ribbon to remove the Styles Gallery

2 The Home Tab

This chapter helps you start entering and manipulating text on the screen. It looks at different ways of editing your work.

Starting a New Document

When you start Word you will be presented with a new, blank document. To create an additional new document:

1 Click the Office Button in the top left of the screen to access its menu, and select New

2 Choose "Blank document" from the options available

3 You now have a blank page ready for new text

Entering and Editing Text

1 Enter a sentence of example text. Do not worry about making mistakes, as these will be easy to correct later on. Watch what happens on the screen as you type. The vertical line, shown below, is your *insertion point*. It indicates where new text will appear

Hot tip

Word automatically works out when to start a new line without breaking words. If you want to force a new line, for example to begin a new paragraph, press the Return or Enter key.

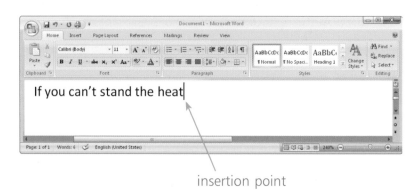

If you can't stand the heat|

insertion point

2 You can move the insertion point using the cursor (arrow) keys, or by clicking a new position with the mouse

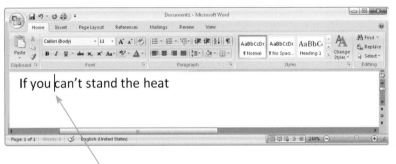

click with the mouse to move the insertion point

3 When the insertion point is in the correct position type some new text. It will appear at the insertion point

4 If you want to start typing at the end of the text again, then make sure you first move the insertion point so that it is to the right of the last character

Don't forget

The words to the right of the insertion point will automatically move along to accommodate any text you are inserting.

23

Beware

Do not be tempted to add extra spacing by pressing the spacebar many times. Although this will work to a certain extent, it's not the most flexible way of controlling spacing. You will learn much better techniques for this in the next chapter.

Deleting Text with the Backspace Key

1 Place the insertion point just after the text you want to delete

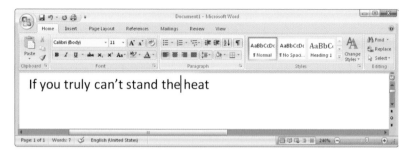

2 Press the Backspace key once to erase the character to the left of the insertion point. Repeat this to continue erasing one character at a time

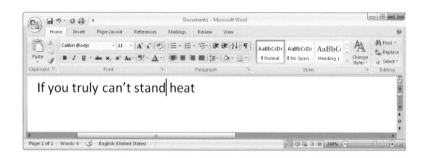

Don't forget

You can use the Undo button in the Quick Access Toolbar, or type Ctrl+Z to restore characters you may have inadvertently deleted.

Deleting Text with the Delete Key

1 This time move the insertion point so that it is just before the text to be deleted

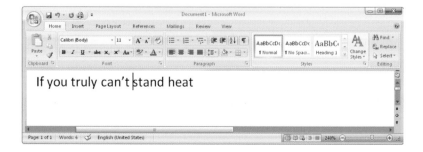

2 Press the Delete key once to erase each character to the *right* of the insertion point

Selecting and Replacing Text

1 Click and drag from left to right across a range of characters to highlight them. If you select the wrong text, click somewhere else to deselect and then try again

2 Anything you now type will automatically replace the currently selected text

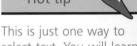

Hot tip

This is just one way to select text. You will learn other ways of doing this in the next chapter.

Click and Type

Provided you are in Print Layout or Web Layout view you can easily add text anywhere on the page.

1 First make sure that Print Layout view is selected from the Page View icons in the Status bar at the bottom of the screen

Page Layout view

2 As you move the mouse over a blank area the pointer icon will indicate to you whether new text will be left-aligned, right-aligned or centered. The example below shows the icon for centered text. Double-click to establish a new insertion point

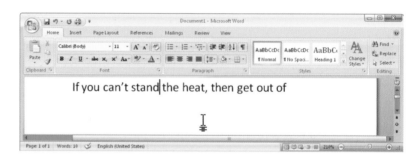

3 Type in some new text

Don't forget

If Click and Type doesn't appear to work open the Office Button menu and choose "Word options". Select Advanced and make sure that the option "Enable click and type" is activated.

26

Hot tip

You will learn more about left, right and centered text in the next chapter.

The Clipboard

The Clipboard is a temporary storage area that can hold text or even other items such as graphic images. It can be used to help you move or copy text you have selected.

Cut and Paste

1 Select the text to be moved. Right-click on the selected text, and then choose Cut

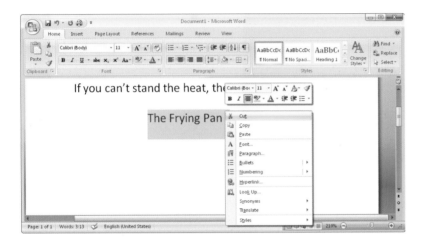

Hot tip

You can also cut and paste using the icons in the Clipboard section of the Home Tab, or with the keyboard shortcuts Ctrl+X and Ctrl+V respectively.

2 The text is removed and placed on the Clipboard. Now place your insertion point at the desired destination, right-click, and then choose Paste

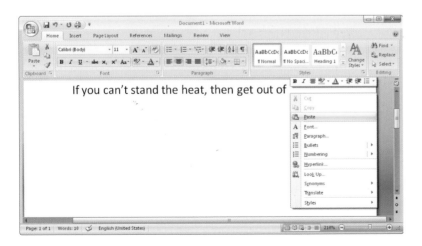

...cont'd

3 Once your text has
next to it. This is th

If you can't stand th

Fr

4 Click on this icon to see the Paste formatting options.
Choose Keep Source Formatting to use the formatting
attributes of the text on the Clipboard

Hot tip

Sometimes you may
want to paste text inside
a larger section of text
that is already formatted
with the correct font,
size and style. To use
the formatting of this
existing section choose
Match Destination
Formatting from the
Paste options.

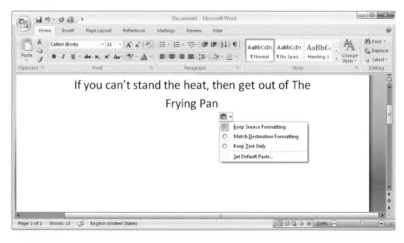

If you can't stand the heat, then get out of The
Frying Pan

5 When you chose Paste, a copy of what was currently on
the Clipboard was placed at the insertion point. You can
paste this text as many times, and in as many locations, as
you like. The Clipboard will contain the same text until
the next time you use Cut or Copy

Copy and Paste

1 Select the text you want to copy and click the Copy icon in the Clipboard area of the Home Tab

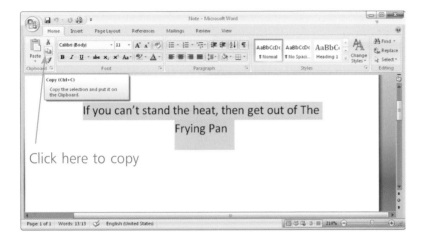

Click here to copy

Don't forget

You can also right-click and choose Copy and Paste from the pop-up menu as illustrated in the previous example. A third way to copy and paste is to use the keyboard shortcuts Ctrl+C and Ctrl+V respectively.

2 Place the insertion point at the destination for the copied text and then click the Paste icon. Alternatively, you can click on the small downward-pointing black triangle under the Paste icon. This will show you additional Paste options

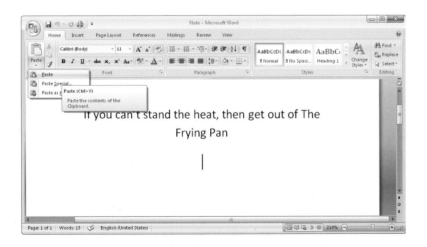

3 For this example choose Paste, the first option

...cont'd

4 As in the Cut and Paste example (page 27), you will see the Paste Options Smart Tag appear beside the new text

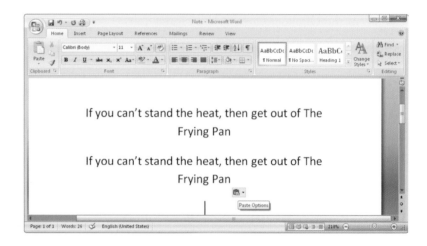

The Spike

The Spike is similar to the Clipboard in that it is a temporary storage area for text. The main difference is that you can add more and more text onto the Spike with a keyboard shortcut.

1 Select some text and type Ctrl+F3. The text disappears. It has been impaled on the Spike

2 Repeat the process with a second piece of text

3 If you want to add even more text to the Spike, then repeat the previous step as many times as you want

4 Finally, position the insertion point at the destination for the text and press Ctrl+Shift+F3. The text is pulled off the Spike and placed back into the document

Hot tip

You can repeat this more times if necessary if you want to collect more pieces of text onto the Spike. Each time you press Ctrl+F3 any selected text is removed from the page and added to the Spike. Note, however, that you only press Ctrl+Shift+F3 once – as soon as the text is back on the page it has been removed from the Spike.

Undo and Redo

1 Use the Undo button in the Quick Access Toolbar, or Ctrl+Z, to undo the last action

2 Alternatively, open the Undo menu, as in the example below, to undo more actions

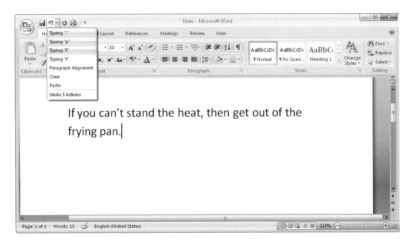

3 To redo the recently undone action, type Ctrl+Y or use the Redo button in the Quick Access Toolbar

4 If the Redo button is grayed out, then there are no more actions that can be redone

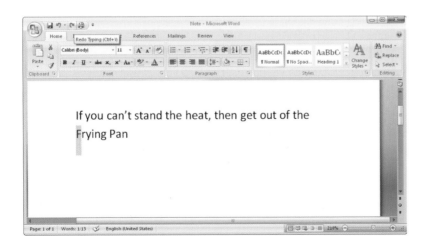

Beware

As soon as you have undone one or more actions, the Redo button becomes active. If you plan to use Redo then you must do it immediately. If you make any new edits before using the Redo button, it will become grayed out again.

Find and Replace

Word can be instructed to search through your document for words, groups of characters, or even formatting attributes.

1 Choose Find from the Editing section of the Home Tab, or type Ctrl+F

2 Enter the search text and then click the Find Next button

3 To replace text choose Replace from the Editing section of the Home Tab, or type Ctrl+H

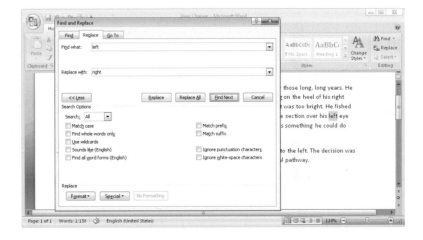

3 Formatting Text

This chapter looks at ways in which you can change the appearance of your text. First you'll see different ways of selecting text. Then you'll learn how to format paragraphs or individual characters.

Selecting Text

Basic Techniques

Selecting text is almost always the first step when formatting or editing, so it is worth knowing all the different techniques. In the previous chapter you saw how to select text by dragging across it with the mouse. This is good for small amounts but is cumbersome when you are trying to select a lot of text.

1 Click an insertion point just to the left of the start of the text you wish to select

2 Now hold down the Shift key and click just to the right of the end of the text to be selected

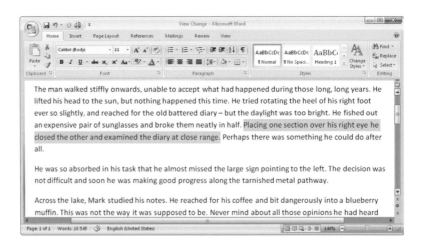

3 If you shift-clicked in the wrong place, try again. The start point of the selection will stay the same – each time you shift-click the end point will move

4 To deselect text, simply click anywhere in the text editing area

5 Double-click directly on a word to select it

6 Triple-click to select an entire paragraph

Discontinuous Text Selection

1 Select some text using any of the previous techniques

2 Now hold down the Control key, click and drag across some text that is separate from your original selection

3 Repeat this process to add more areas to your selection

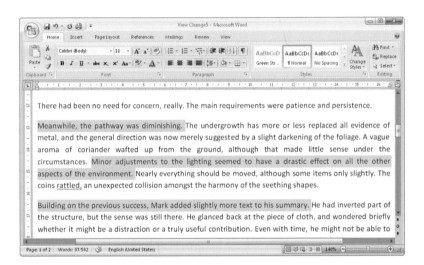

Selection with the Alt Key

If you click and drag while holding the Alt key down you can select all text in a rectangular area. This is less useful than it appears.

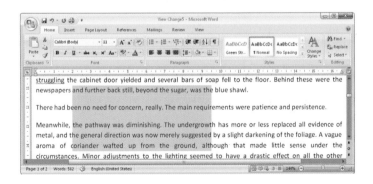

...cont'd

Using the Left Margin Area

1 Move your mouse into the left margin area. You can tell that you are in the correct area if the cursor turns into an arrow pointing to the right instead of to the left

2 Drag vertically to select whole lines of text

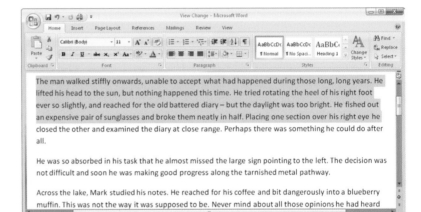

Selecting Text with Similar Formatting

1 Select a small sample in the format you want

2 Open the Select menu in the Editing section of the Home Tab and choose the option "Select Text with Similar Formatting"

Selecting Hidden Characters

1 Make sure the Show Paragraph Mark ¶ option is active. This is in the Paragraph section of the Home Tab

2 You will see the place where you pressed the Return key (to start a new paragraph) as a ¶ symbol. A single centered dot represents a space. It is now easy to see whether or not you have these characters selected

3 Finally switch off the Show Paragraph Mark option

If you go to the Office Button menu and choose Word Options and then Advanced, you'll see several useful settings. If "Use smart paragraph selection" is active Word will automatically select the ¶ character at the end of the paragraph – regardless of whether is hidden.

"Use smart paragraph selection" can be helpful as it makes it easier to cut and paste paragraphs without unsightly blank lines appearing in your document.

Character-Level Formatting

Formatting with the Mini Toolbar

We saw in Chapter 1 that the Mini Toolbar allows you to adjust the appearance of your text in many useful ways.

1 Select the text you wish to format. As you move your mouse near the selected area the Mini Toolbar will become visible

2 Open the font menu in the Mini Toolbar. The menu list is previewed using the fonts themselves. Recently used fonts are listed near the top

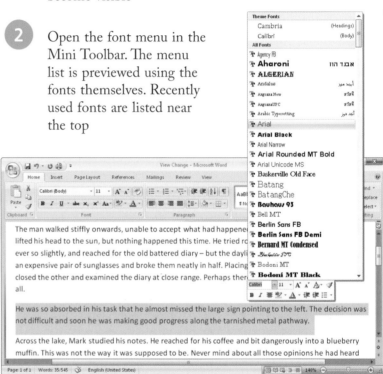

3 Character-level formatting covers any settings that can affect individual characters (as opposed to a setting such as centered alignment, which works at the paragraph rather than the character level). The Mini Toolbar's controls for character-level formatting include font size, bold and italic effects, text and background color

4 As soon as you move away from the text the Mini Toolbar disappears again

Formatting with the Home Tab

The Font section of the Home Tab gives you access to more ways of controlling the appearance of characters.

1 Select some text. Change font, size, and other attributes by selecting from the Font section in the Home Tab

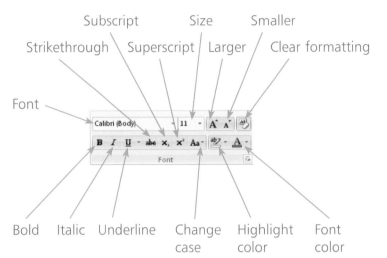

Subscript   Size   Smaller

Strikethrough \ Superscript / Larger / Clear formatting

Font

Bold   Italic   Underline   Change   Highlight   Font
                            case   color   color

39

2 Whenever you select text the Font area will show you its current settings (if there are mixed settings within the text you've selected then the value will show as blank)

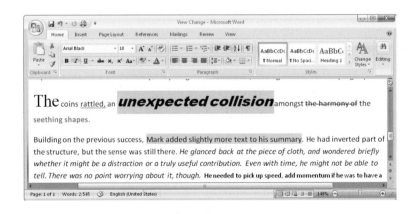

...cont'd

The Font Dialog

You can call up the Font dialog box to get full character-level control over the appearance of your text.

1 Select some text. Click on the dialog icon in the lower right corner of the Font area of the Home Tab, or press Ctrl+D

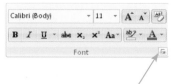

Open font dialog

2 You now have access to additional effects, such as double strikethrough and shadow, outline, emboss and engrave effects

3 Click on the Character Spacing page to control the precise positioning and scaling of the selected characters

4 Kerning is a process used to adjust the space between certain combinations of characters. For example, when the letters "T" and "o" occur next to each other, normal spacing appears too wide. If you activate kerning then they will be brought closer together to create the illusion of normal spacing

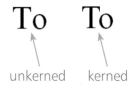

unkerned   kerned

Beware

Scaling allows you to stretch or compress text horizontally. While this can sometimes work well for large titles it is not recommended for use on main text, as the results are often unreadable. If you need narrower or wider text then try using a different font that is already the desired shape.

Don't forget

Since kerning can slow down screen redrawing you might want to switch it off altogether or activate it only for larger font sizes (where spacing is more noticable).

Paragraph-Level Formatting

The Mini Toolbar gives you the ability to switch centering on and off, adjust the left indent or create a bulleted list. For most paragraph-level attributes, however, you will use the Paragraph section of the Home Tab.

Alignment

1 If you want to change just one paragraph then simply click anywhere within it. If you want to change multiple paragraphs then select them using any of the techniques we looked at earlier

2 Click on one of the alignment icons to choose left, centered, right or justified alignment. There is an example of each type illustrated below

Don't forget

Remember that a heading is regarded by Word as a single-line paragraph.

41

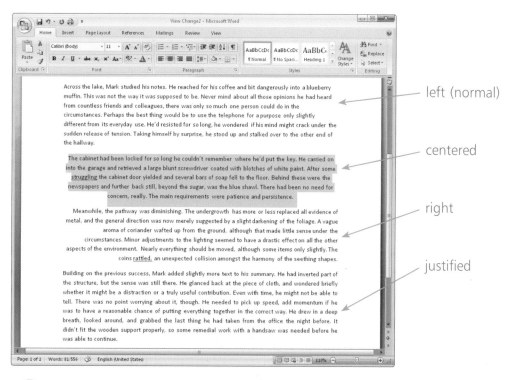

left (normal)

centered

right

justified

3 To see more paragraph controls, click the small open dialog icon ▣ in the lower right corner of this section

...cont'd

Bulleted Lists

1 Enter the text for your list, pressing the Return key after each item. Select this text

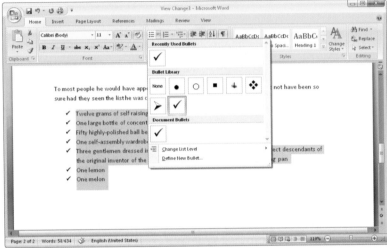

Hot tip

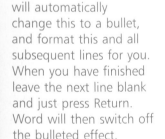

A quick way to create a bulleted list is to type an asterisk at the beginning of the first line. Word will automatically change this to a bullet, and format this and all subsequent lines for you. When you have finished leave the next line blank and just press Return. Word will then switch off the bulleted effect.

2 Open the Bullets pop-up menu in the Paragraph area of the Home Tab

3 Select the desired type of bullet. If you don't like any of those on offer then choose Define New Bullet...

Hot tip

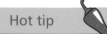

From the Define New Bullet dialog you can choose any image or character from a font to be used as a bullet. Many fonts, such as Wingdings and Dingbats, are pictorial – this makes them a good source for bullets.

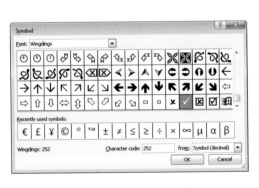

Numbered Lists

1 If you enter, on a new line, text beginning with a "1." then Word will automatically create a numbered list. When you press Return the next numbered line will be created for you

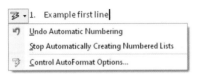

2 This behavior may not always be what you want. If it is not, then click on the AutoCorrect icon that appears by your text. You can then undo the automatic numbering just for this example, or disable the feature for future lists

3 If you choose Control AutoFormat Options... you will call up a dialog with settings for this plus many other automatic features

4 Another way to create a numbered list is to enter your text with no numbers, and then select it in the normal way and open the Numbering pop-up menu in the Paragraph section of the Home Tab

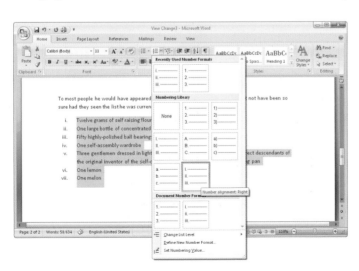

Customized Numbered Lists

1 Select your list, open the Numbering pop-up menu in the Paragraph section of the Home Tab, and choose Define New Number Format...

2 Choose the Number style, format and alignment, and click the Font button if you want to use a different font for the numbers themselves

Multilevel Lists

1 Create the text for your list. Press the Tab key at the beginning of a line once for each level of indent

2 Open the Multilevel pop-up menu in the Paragraph section and select the desired style

Hot tip

You can also customize your multilevel lists by choosing Define New Multilevel List... from the Multilevel pop-up menu.

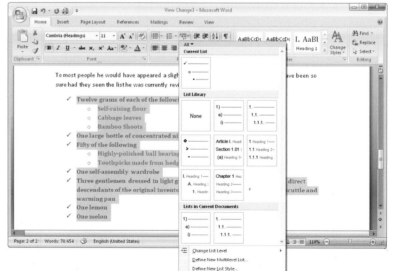

Quick Styles

Styles help you to apply a consistent set of formatting attributes to main text, headings and other elements of your document. Once you start using styles you'll be able to control your document's presentation with the minimum of tedious manual editing.

Word comes with a set of styles for you to use straight away, but it's also easy to create your own. There are two main types of style:

Paragraph Styles

These can contain information about virtually any text attribute, e.g. font, size, alignment, spacing and color. They are called paragraph styles because they are applied at the paragraph level.

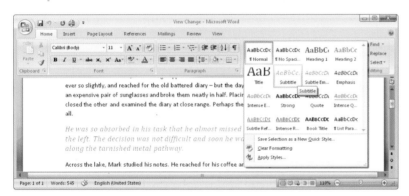

Don't forget

A paragraph of text can only have a maximum of one paragraph style applied to it at any time. If you select a single word and apply a paragraph style to it, then the whole of the surrounding paragraph will be affected.

45

Character Styles

These can contain information about character-level attributes only, e.g. font and size, but not alignment (which is a paragraph-level attribute). They can be applied to any amount of text, even individual characters or words.

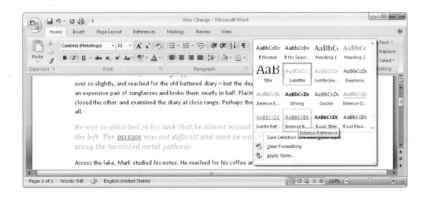

Hot tip

There is a third type known as a Linked Style. This can contain both character and paragraph level attributes. See page 58 "Linked Styles" for more about this.

...cont'd

Creating a Style

1 The easiest way to create a new style is to select some text that already has all, or most, of the attributes you want to use

2 Open the Style Gallery by clicking the icon in the lower right corner of the example styles in the Styles area of the Home Tab

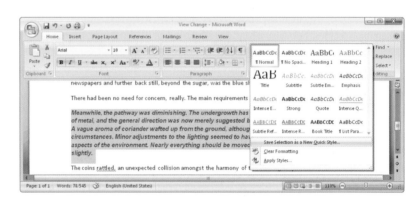

3 In the dialog that appears give the style a name

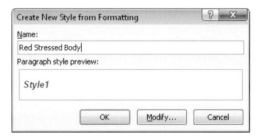

4 Note that the dialog also shows you a preview of the style you are about to create. If this does not look correct then click the Cancel button and examine the text you selected. If necessary alter its formatting or select a different sample of text

5 If you are already happy with the style's attributes then click OK; otherwise select Modify... to alter the settings

Modifying a Style using the Dialog Box

1 Locate the style in the Style Gallery or the main Styles area, right-click and select Modify...

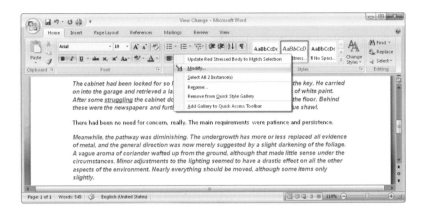

Hot tip

Another way to modify a Style is to type Ctrl+Shift+S. The Apply Styles window will appear – type the first few letters of the Style's name. If the desired style appears then click the Modify... button; if not then select from the list and click Modify...

2 The following dialog appears. From here you can rename the style or alter attributes such as font, size or effects such as bold and italics

Many other useful settings can be made from this dialog. If you click the Format button, you can access dialogs for Font, Paragraph, Tabs and several other categories.

3 When you are happy with your settings click OK

47

...cont'd

Don't forget

If you are not happy with the changes you made then you can always use the Undo button in the Quick Access Toolbar or type Ctrl+Z.

Beware

Changing style sets will drastically alter your document, so you may want to make a backup copy (using the Office Button menu's Save As... option) before you use this feature.

4 Any text in your document to which this style was applied will be automatically updated

The Change Styles Button

If you've been using Word's built-in styles, or if you've created your own using the same names, then you can switch the style set to redesign your document completely.

1 Click the Change Styles button in the Styles section of the Home Tab to access its pop-up menu

2 Select one of the options from the Style Set submenu

3 Each style in the style set will replace the style of the same name in your current document

Modifying a Style using Document Text

One problem with modifying styles via the dialog box is that you do not see the results of your changes until you return to the main document. Here is another way of editing a style, which does not suffer from this drawback:

1 Select some text that already uses the style you want to modify

2 Make formatting changes directly to this, using the techniques you have learned so far. In this example the font, size and spacing have been altered

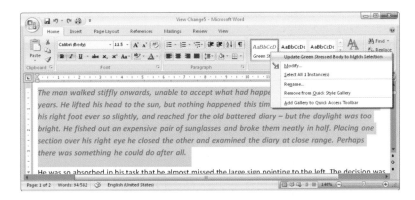

3 Right-click on the style name in the Styles section of the Home Tab and choose the "Update ... to Match Selection" option

4 The style's definition will be modified. All other document text that uses this style will be changed automatically

Beware

When following these steps, make sure you click the right mouse button rather than the left. Left-clicking will reset the selected text to the original style definition. If you do this accidentally then use the Undo button, or Ctrl+Z, and try again.

The Ruler

Text that is laid out neatly with accurate horizontal positioning greatly helps to give your documents a professional look. Effective use of white space, including tabulation, is the key to this.

Making the Ruler Visible

 1 Move your pointer to the very top of the editing area, and then move upwards so that you have just touched the lower border of the Tab controls area. The ruler will appear temporarily

Left indent for the first line of each paragraph

Left indent for subsequent lines

Drag here to move both left indents at once

Right indent

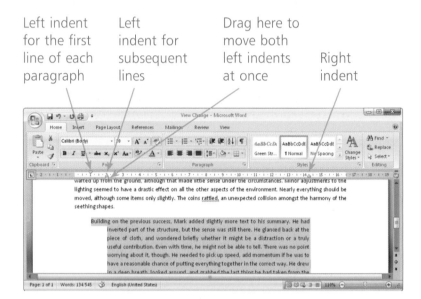

2 Experiment by moving the left and right indent markers on the Ruler and observe what happens on the page. It helps if you have several lines of text selected

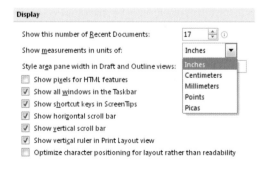

Tabulation

Tab stops are paragraph-level attributes that define what happens when the Tab key is pressed when entering text. If you select a paragraph and examine the Ruler you will see any tab stops that have been defined. If no tab stops have been defined for this paragraph then the default tabs apply. These are marked in the Ruler as small vertical lines, spaced out at regular intervals in its lower section.

Overriding Default Tabulation

1 Click the Show/Hide ¶ button in the Paragraph section of the Home Tab. This will allow you to see where you've pressed the Tab key – shown as a small arrow pointing rightwards

Don't forget

When you click the Show/Hide ¶ button paragraph marks also appear visibly as the ¶ character.

2 Type in some text similar to the example below. Note that each text element is separated from the next by a Tab character. Do not worry about how far across the screen the Tab takes you: this will be altered soon. Make sure you only press Tab once between one element and the next

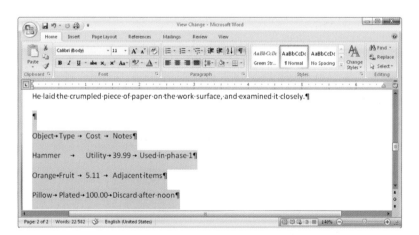

3 Also make sure that you press Return once at the end of each line. This will show up as a ¶ character as in the illustration above

4 Now select all your newly-entered text

...cont'd

5 Now make sure that the ⌐ icon is visible at the left side of the Ruler. This means that when you create a tab stop it will use left alignment. If it looks different, then click on it until it changes to the correct symbol

6 Now click in the Ruler around the 1 inch mark to create a new left tab. Once it is created you can drag it left or right to adjust its position

52

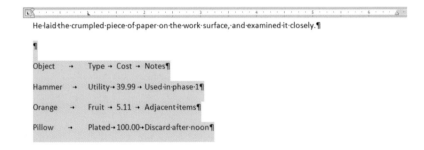

7 The text should move so that the character following the first tab lines up vertically. Making sure that your text is still selected, create some more tab stops

8 As you create and move tab stops, note that the text automatically moves to follow your new design

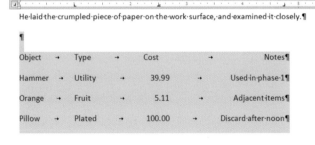

9 Experiment by creating more tabs. You can also delete tabs by dragging them upwards or downwards out of the Ruler

10 You can call up the Tabs dialog by double-clicking directly on any tab

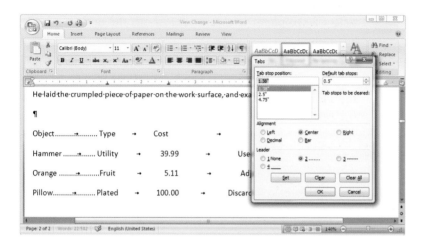

Don't forget

Tabulation can be built into a style definition, and so used consistently throughout a document.

11 Select a tab from the list on the left. You can now change its type, add a leader (as in the above example, which leads into the first tab with a series of dots), set new tabs, or clear tabs

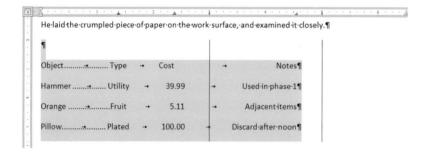

12 In the above example bar tabs were created at 3 inches and 5 inches. These create vertical lines

13 When you are done, click the Show/Hide ¶ button in the Paragraph section of the Home Tab. This makes the hidden characters invisible again so that you get a better idea of the appearance of the final result

The Format Painter

The Format Painter gives a very easy way to copy attributes from one place to another.

1 Select a sample of text that already has the desired attributes

2 Click the Format Painter icon in the Clipboard section of the Home Tab. This "loads" the icon with the attributes of the selected text

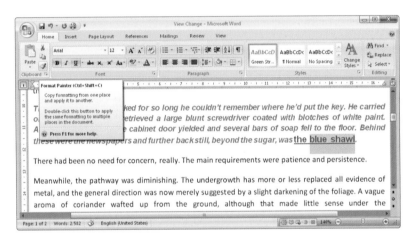

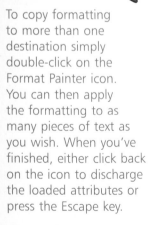

Hot tip

To copy formatting to more than one destination simply double-click on the Format Painter icon. You can then apply the formatting to as many pieces of text as you wish. When you've finished, either click back on the icon to discharge the loaded attributes or press the Escape key.

3 Note that your mouse pointer has changed to show that you have attributes loaded. Now use it to drag across your target text. The attributes are applied to the text

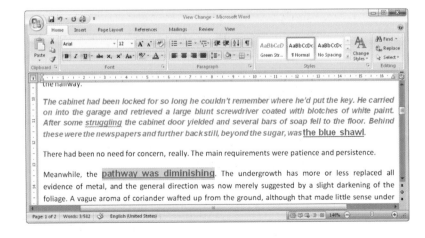

Paragraph-Level Styles

You can create more advanced types of style from the Styles
window.

1 Open the Styles window by clicking on the  icon in the
bottom right corner of the Styles area of the Home Tab

2 You will see a list of recommended styles

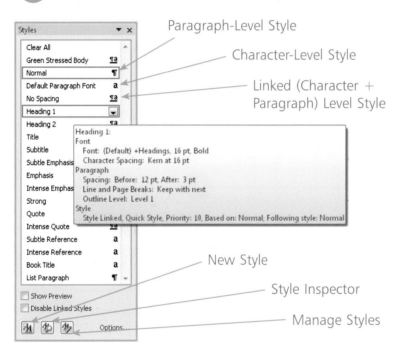

Paragraph-Level Style

Character-Level Style

Linked (Character +
Paragraph) Level Style

New Style

Style Inspector

Manage Styles

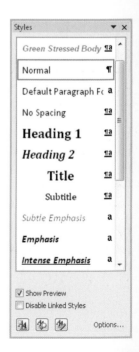

55

3 If you allow your mouse to hover over a particular style
name, a summary box will appear. This lists the essential
attributes of the style

4 Click on Options... to select
which styles should be
shown in the Styles window.
You can also control how
they are displayed and sorted

...cont'd

Creating a New Paragraph-Level Style

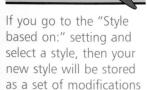

Hot tip

If you go to the "Style based on:" setting and select a style, then your new style will be stored as a set of modifications to the selected style.

For example, you may create a style called "Body Text smaller" based on a style "Body Text". If you set the size attribute to be, say, 9 points, then the style is stored as "9 point, based on Body Text".

Later on, if you modify the style "Body Text" to use a different font, color and size, then "Body Text smaller" will automatically inherit all the new attributes except for size (which is overridden by its own definition).

1 Open the Styles window

2 Click the New Style button, located at the bottom of the window

3 Enter a name for the style

4 For "Style type" select Paragraph

5 Select the other formatting options as appropriate

6 If you need access to the full set of style attributes, click the Format button

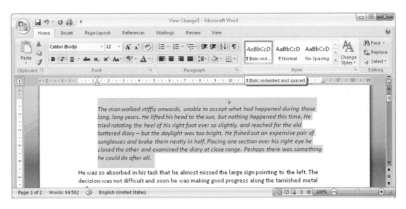

7 Click OK when you're done

8 Your new style is now available in the Styles section of the Home Tab. Note the ¶ symbol next to its name – this indicates that the style works at the paragraph level

Character-Level Styles

Creating a New Character-Level Style

1 Open the Styles window

2 Click the New Style button, located at the bottom of the window. As before, give your style a name

3 For "Style type" select Character

4 Select the other formatting options as appropriate. Note that, because you are creating a character style, you do not have access to paragraph attributes such as alignment

5 Click the Format button to access additional attributes

6 Click OK when you're done

7 Your new style is now available in the Styles section of the Home Tab. If you open the Styles window you will see the **a** symbol next to its name – this indicates that the style works at the character level

Hot tip

Once you've created a style and clicked OK, you can no longer change its style type. For example, if you create a character-level style called "greentext1" you cannot change it into a paragraph style.

However it is easy to create a paragraph style using the same attributes. Simply select "greentext1" in the Styles window and then click the New Style button.

Linked Styles

A linked style can be used at either the paragraph or the character level, depending on the amount of text selected when it's applied.

Creating a New Linked Style

1 Open the Style window and click the New Style button

2 Give your style a name. For "Style type" select "Linked (paragraph and character)"

3 Select the other formatting options as appropriate

4 If you need access to the full set of style attributes, click the Format button

5 Click OK when you're done

6 Select a whole paragraph of text (the quickest way to do this is to triple-click anywhere inside the paragraph), locate your new style in the Home Tab and apply it

If you apply a linked style to a paragraph then all its attributes are used. However, if you apply it to a smaller section of text only its character-level attributes are used. For example, if the linked style is centered then that form of alignment is only used if you apply the style to a whole paragraph or paragraphs.

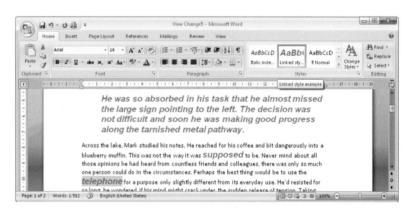

7 Now select an individual word in a different paragraph and apply the style

Mixing Styles in a Paragraph

Character-level and paragraph-level styles can be used in the same paragraph. In this case the character-level style's attributes take precedence. The following example is a good illustration of this.

1 Select an entire paragraph and apply a paragraph-level style to it. In this example a style called "Green stressed body" was used. It is Arial, 10 point, green, italic, centered text

2 Now select a small group of words within the paragraph and apply a character-level style. Here we have used a style called "Blue underline char style", which is 12 point, underlined and blue. The style definition has no font name built in so the font remains the same as that for "Green stressed body"

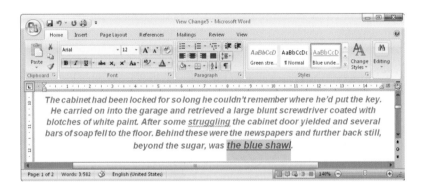

3 Note that the character-level style's attributes override those of the paragraph-level style

4 Now, with the same group of words selected, manually adjust the size to make it larger – 14 point in the following example

5 Now open the Styles window and click on the Style Inspector icon:

Don't forget

The selected words in this example still follow the attributes of the paragraph style, except where they have been overridden by the character-level style. So, if you edited "Green stressed body" so that its font was Times New Roman this would affect all the text. If, however, you made "Green stressed body" a darker green color, the example text seen highlighted here would still be blue.

...cont'd

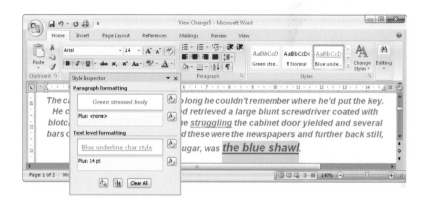

This shows you exactly how the text was formatted.

It is sometimes tempting not to bother with styles, and instead to do all your text formatting with the Mini Toolbar and the Font section within the Home Tab.

While this is initially quicker, it can make life harder in the long term. As your documents grow you will soon want to make sure your formatting and overall design is (a) consistent and (b) easy to change without lots of tedious reselecting and formatting of text.

Formatting text via styles brings you both of these advantages.

Reformatting the Entire Document

If you format your documents using a set of styles with standard names, then you have the potential to redesign everything radically with just a few mouse clicks.

Here are two examples. The document is exactly the same, except that the Change Styles button was used to select a different Style Set in each case.

4 Working with a Document

This chapter helps you to work with a document. It looks at scrolling, zooming and storing on disk. You'll also see how to start a new document by using a predesigned template.

Scrolling

When your text is too large for the document window, you'll need to use one of the following navigation methods:

The scroll boxes' positions let you know where you are in a document. For example, when the vertical scroll box is at the top of the scroll bar you are looking at the top (the beginning) of the document.

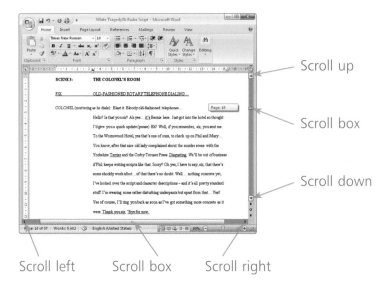

Scroll up

Scroll box

Scroll down

Scroll left   Scroll box   Scroll right

As you scroll down, the scroll box moves like an elevator down a shaft. The size of the box indicates how much of the document you are currently viewing. For example, if the box occupies one third of the scroll bar, then you're viewing a third of the total document.

Quick Ways to Scroll

1 Drag the scroll box directly to a new position

2 Click in the scroll bar to either side of the scroll box. The document will immediately scroll in that direction one screen at a time

3 As you move your insertion point with the arrow (cursor) keys, Word will scroll so that it can always be seen

4 If your mouse has a wheel, this can usually be used to scroll vertically through your document

5 The PgUp (Page Up) and PgDn (Page Down) keys will move you up and down one screen at a time

Browsing

Near the bottom of the vertical scroll bar, on the right edge of the main window, are the browse icons.

Go to previous object

Select browse object

Go to next object

Initially the item type is set to Page. This means the "Go to previous object" button works as "Previous page", and "Go to next object" is "Next page". If you hover over the icons with your mouse, "Previous page" and "Next page" will show as tooltips.

Browsing using Different Types of Object

1 Click on the "Select browse object" button. The following options will appear:

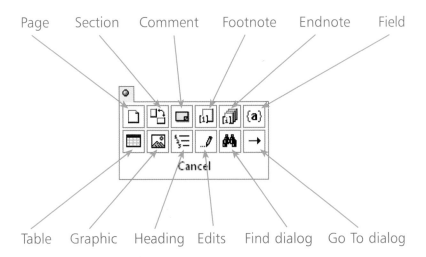

Page   Section   Comment   Footnote   Endnote   Field

Table   Graphic   Heading   Edits   Find dialog   Go To dialog

2 Click on any icon to select the type of object to browse

3 The "Previous object" and "Next object" buttons will now change to reflect your selection. For example, if you clicked on the Heading icon, then the buttons will now act as "Previous heading" and "Next heading"

63

Zooming

Zooming allows you to control the level of magnification on screen. The controls for this are in the bottom right corner.

Hot tip

See Chapter 11: "The View Tab" for more ways to zoom.

Current magnification   Zoom out   Adjust zoom level   Zoom in

The Zoom Dialog Box

1 Click on the "Current magnification" icon to open the Zoom dialog box

2 Choose one of the options, or enter a percentage value directly and then click OK

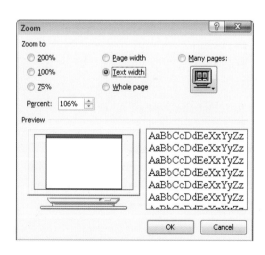

Saving a Document

A quick way to save is to click the Save icon in the Quick Access Toolbar. Word will save your document to disk using the current file name.

Save icon ————

Another way of doing this is to choose Save from the Office Button menu.

Using Save As

This gives you greater control over how you save, allowing you to specify file name, type, location and other options.

1 Open the Office Button menu and click Save As. A submenu appears

2 Choose the option Word Document to save in the default format for the current version of Word

Hot tip

The keyboard shortcut for Save is Ctrl+S.

Hot tip

See Chapter 12: "Advanced Features" for more information about the file formats available to you when you save your document, and Chapter 5: "Printing and Publishing" for details on exporting in PDF or XPS format.

...cont'd

White Tragedy8b Radio Script

3 The following dialog appears

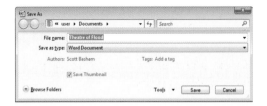

4 Click the Browse Folders button to expand the dialog

5 Navigate to the desired directory, making sure the filename is correct

6 If you click the Tools button and choose Save Options... you will be taken to the Save section of the Word Options dialog box

7 Click OK to dismiss the Options dialog, and then Save when you are happy with the settings

Opening a Document

Before starting Word, if you locate a Word document and double-click on it then Windows will launch Word automatically and open the file for editing.

Opening a Document from within Word

1 Open the Office Button menu and choose Open, or press Ctrl+O. The following dialog appears:

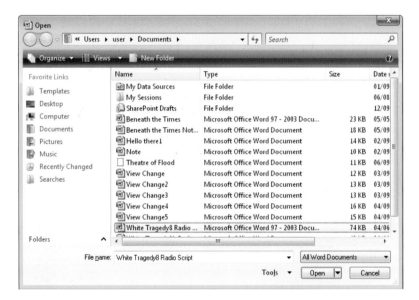

2 By default you will be shown all the Word documents in the current directory. If necessary, use the standard Windows controls to navigate to a different directory/folder

3 Word can open a wide range of other file types. To see these open the pop-up menu on the button marked All Word Documents and select the desired file type

Hot tip

Normally you would just click the Open button to start working on the selected document. If you click the downward-pointing arrow on the Open button, however, you can choose more options. You could, for example, decide to open the document in Read-Only mode.

Earlier Versions of Word

Word 2007 can open documents created in earlier versions, back to Word 97. If you do this, then you will be operating in compatibility mode – this means that the range of features available will be restricted to those that allow the document to be saved in the earlier file format.

Editing an Older Document Type

1 Locate and open the file in the normal way. In the main window title bar you'll see the document name followed by the words Compatibility Mode in square brackets

2 When you have finished editing the document, choose Save As from the Office Button menu

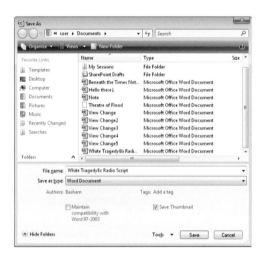

Don't forget

If you save with the "Maintain compatibility..." option switched off then you will change the document to a Word 2007 version. You will be able to use all the new features of Word 2007, but you will have lost the ability to open the document in an older version of Word.

3 Select the option "Maintain compatibility with Word 97-2003" to keep the file format the same. This means that you will be able to open and edit the document on a computer that has the earlier version of Word installed. If the option is deselected the following dialog appears:

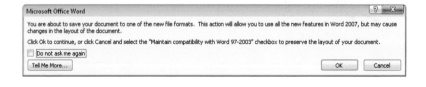

Finding Documents

The Open dialog also has a feature allowing automatic searching based on filename.

1 Type Ctrl+O or click Open in the Office Button menu

2 Navigate to the folder you wish to search using the standard Windows controls. Word will be able to search this including all its sub-folders

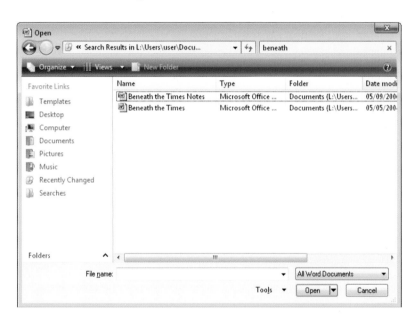

3 Enter the search text in the field in the top right corner of the dialog. In this example the search word is "beneath"

4 As soon as you have entered the search text, Word will show you all filenames that contain your text. Note that you did not need to enter the whole file name – just a part is sufficient

Hot tip

If you are unsure about the precise filename you can use a question mark to indicate a single unknown character, and an asterisk to indicate an unknown sequence of zero or more characters. For example, "w?nd" will match words such as "wind", "wend" and "wand". "B*th" would match words such as "bath", "both" and "beneath". Searching is case-insensitive, so you do not need to worry about use of capital letters.

Don't forget

If you cannot find your file using this method, then try using the Windows Search feature instead. Its Advanced option lets you search using name, date, size, file type and also combinations of these.

Creating a New Document

Earlier on we saw how to create a new blank document. Here we will look at other options to give you more of a head start, using document templates where some of the work has already been done for you.

Accessing Microsoft Office Online

1 Open the Office Button menu and choose New

2 Click on the Featured option, which is within the section called Microsoft Office Online

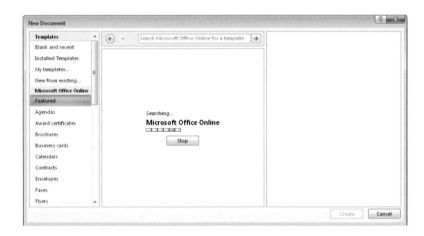

3 Once the online search has completed, you can browse through any of the online categories:

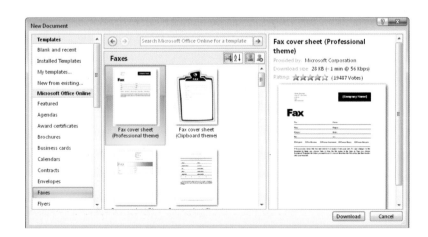

4 If you decide to download a new document template, you may see the following message:

 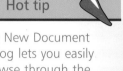
5 Click Continue and Microsoft will validate your installation of Microsoft Office

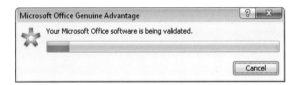

6 Once this is done your document will open. You can now edit and add to the sample text, which has already been positioned and formatted for you

...cont'd

New from Existing Document

The installed templates are accessible from the New Document dialog, and will create a new copy of themselves when selected.

You can also use an ordinary document in a similar way:

1 Open the Office Button menu and choose New

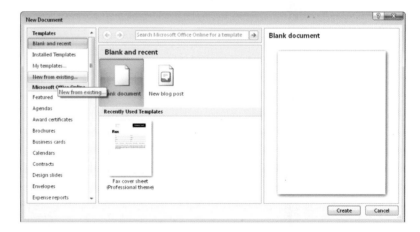

2 Choose "New from existing..." and then select the document you wish to use. A new document will be created based on a copy of this

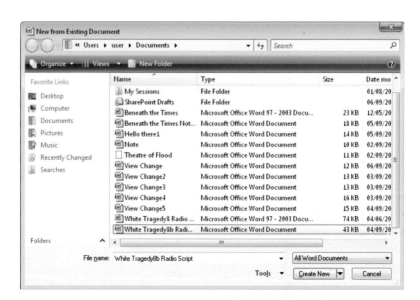

5 Printing and Publishing

This chapter looks at PDF and XPS. These are formats that allow you to distribute your documents to a wide audience.

Printing

Before you print a document you may wish to check it on screen, in order to eliminate any errors that were not spotted earlier. Word offers a Print Preview facility, which shows you pages exactly as they will print, with none of the modifications made by the normal Word views.

Accessing Print Preview

1 Open the Office Button menu, choose Print and then choose Print Preview from the submenu

2 The Print Preview Command Tab appears. In the Zoom area there are controls to call up the Zoom dialog, Zoom to 100%, or scale to show one or two pages at a time

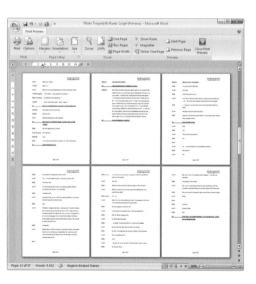

3 You can also use the normal zoom controls in the bottom right corner of the screen to zoom in and out more flexibly

4 The Preview area of the Print Preview tab allows you to show or hide the Ruler, activate the Magnifier (which turns your mouse pointer into a magnifying glass icon), or move easily between pages. The Shrink One Page control will attempt to reduce the document length by one page. It does this by adjusting the size and spacing of the text

5 When you are finished with Print Preview, click the Close Print Preview button at the right-hand side of the Preview area of the Print Preview Tab. Alternatively you can go ahead and print directly without closing down Print Preview. To do this click on Print or Print Options (described below) in the Print area

The Print Dialog

Usually you will want to review the print settings before you actually print your document.

1 Open the Office Button menu and choose Print

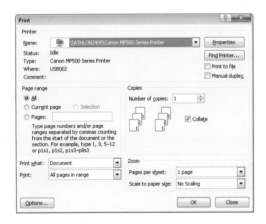

2 Select the printer, choose a page range and number of copies. You can also scale to a particular paper size

3 Click OK to print or Close to return to the main screen

4 Your document will now be printed. There may be a delay while the data is prepared and then transferred to the printer

75

Publishing a Blog

The word "blog" comes from "web log". It is a shared online journal that allows users to publish any type of information, opinions or diaries.

To set up your own blog you need an account with a blog service provider. There are a number of free services mentioned in Word's Help pages – in the following example we'll use Windows Live Spaces, which is a free service provided by Microsoft.

Setting up a Blog Account

1 Start your browser and enter the following URL into its address bar:

http://spaces.live.com

2 Click on the button "Create your space". You will now be asked to sign into Windows Live, if you have not already done so. If you are not yet a member of Windows Live follow the instructions to create a new account (this is a free service)

Create your Windows Live Space

With your own space, you can share your thoughts and interests with just your friends and family, or with everyone. You can set up your own blog, profile, friends list, photo albums, music lists, and more.

* **Required field**

Enter a title for your space

* Title: The Anti-Caking Agents Space

Enter a name to include in your Spaces web address

*http:// AntiCakingAgents .spaces.live.com/

Check availability

Your use of Windows Live Spaces is subject to the Windows Live terms of use.

Create   Cancel

3 Enter a title for your space and a name that will become part of its web address. It is important that this is unique within the site, so try to choose something that no one else has already created. You can click the "Check availability" button to test this

4 Click the Create button. The next screen looks like this:

You've created your space

Your space is located at:
http://AntiCakingAgents.spaces.live.com/

Your permissions are currently set to **Everyone**   Change Permissions

Permissions allow you to decide who can view your space and your profile information.

- Everyone: Provides access to anyone on the Web. Permissions for your space need to be set to Everyone if you want to syndicate your space, have your space displayed in the New and Updated modules, notify ping servers, or allow trackbacks on your blog.
- Messenger: Provides access only to people in your Messenger allow list.
- Messenger & friends: Provides access only to people in your Messenger allow list and your friends list.
- Messenger, friends & friends of your friends: Provides access only to people on your Messenger allow list, your friends list, your mutual friends, and their mutual friends.
- Custom: Customize your permissions list by selecting which groups of people can see your space.

Please be advised that spaces that do not conform to the code of conduct will be taken down and illegal content reported to authorities.

> Go to your space

5 Click "Go to your space", Options (top right of the screen) and then "E-mail publishing" (left edge of screen)

Options
Space settings
Permissions
Blog settings
E-mail publishing
Storage
Statistics
Communication preferences

💾 Save   ✕ Cancel

You can publish blog entries and photos to your space from any device that can send e-mail, such as a computer or mobile device. **Important:** Your mobile carrier may charge a fee to send e-mail from your mobile device. For more information, contact your mobile carrier.

☑ Turn on e-mail publishing.

Post to your space from e-mail or mobile device.
You can use up to three e-mail addresses, including e-mail sent from a mobile device, to publish blog entries or post photos to your space. Only entries sent from these e-mail addresses will be published to your blog.

E-mail address 1: ron_doo_ron@hotmail.c
E-mail address 2:
E-mail address 3:

Example: yourname@example.com

Tip: If you don't know your device's e-mail address, send a test e-mail to the e-mail address you used to set up your space. The "from" field displays your devices e-mail address.

Send your posts to this e-mail address.
Type a secret word that contains five to ten letters and numbers. It cannot have spaces or symbols.

Enter a secret word: temppw

Send your posts here.
To making e-mail publishing easier, add this e-mail address to your contacts or address book.

E-mail address:

anticakingagents.temppw@spaces.live.com

Important: To help keep your space secure, don't share this e-mail address.

Select your publishing settings.

⦿ **Save entries as drafts.** (recommended)
Select this option if you want to sign in to your space and review entries before they're published. This option can help keep your space secure.

◯ **Publish entries immediately.**
Select this option if you want entries published to your space immediately after being received by your space.

💾 Save   ✕ Cancel

Don't forget

Make a note of the location of your new space. In our example the URL:

http://AntiCakingAgents. spaces.live.com

is what your friends will use to see what you have written.

Hot tip

You can update your blog directly from this website, or by manually emailing from one of the three email addresses you specify. In this chapter, however, we will concentrate on how you can configure Word to publish new blog entries automatically for you.

...cont'd

6 Check the box "Turn on e-mail publishing"

7 Enter at least one email address in the area provided, and give a secret word consisting of between five and ten letters or numbers. Using this information Word will be able to write to your blog

8 Close down your browser and return to Word. You are now ready to create a document that will be your first blog entry. From the Office Button menu choose New

9 In the Templates section, the first item "Blank and recent" should already be highlighted – if not then select it now. Choose "New blog post"

If you have already registered your blog account then these steps will be missed out and you will be taken straight to the new blog document. In this case you might want to click the Open Existing button in the Blog area of the Blog Post command tab. This will allow you to open an existing blog so that you can add new text.

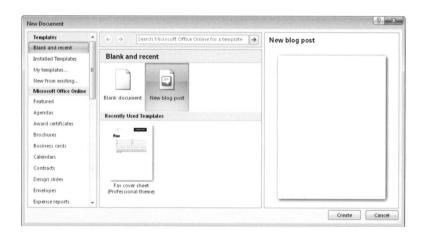

If this is the first time you've using blogging you'll need to let Word know where your blog is and how to send information to it.

10 Click the Register Now button

The following dialog box appears:

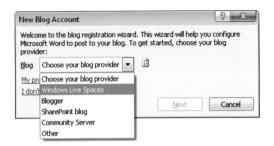

11 For Blog, choose Windows Live Spaces

12 Now enter your space name exactly as you did earlier. Then enter your secret word and select the option Remember Secret Word

13 Click OK. You should see the following confirmation:

14 Click OK to dismiss the message and start working on your new blog post. The new document opens in Web Layout view, which gives you a better idea of how your blog will look when it's published to the Web

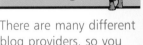

Don't forget

There are many different blog providers, so you might want to research several before deciding on which one to use.

...cont'd

15 You can now work on your blog entry. Click on the field labelled [Enter Post Title Here] and type in your title. Then add the main text below the horizontal line

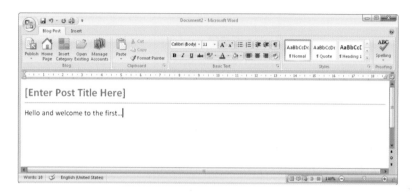

16 Continue adding text, using any of the formatting controls available. You might want to run the Spelling Checker (see Chapter 10) before posting the blog entry

17 Blog entries can be associated with a category. To do this click the Insert Category button in the Blog Post Tab

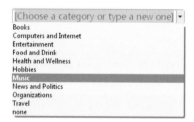

A Category field is added below the title.

18 Select a category from the list, or type directly into the field to create a new category

19 Carry on working on your blog. You can save this as a normal document and return to it later if need be. When you are ready you can instruct Word to update the blog online

Posting to Your Blog

If you are happy with the text, you are ready to post to the blog.

1 If necessary open your document and check that you are ready to publish. Make sure that you are still connected to the Internet

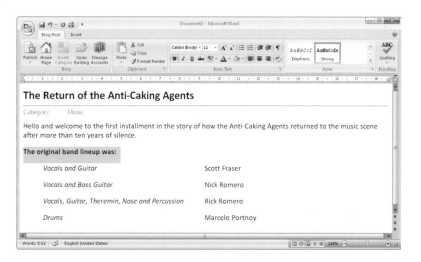

2 Click the Publish button in the Blog Post Command Tab

This post was republished to The Anti-Caking Agents Space at 21:37:38 09/09/2007

The above confirmation message will appear at the top of your document.

You can now go to your browser – enter the URL you noted earlier to access your space and check your updated blog.

Converting to PDF

Adobe's PDF (Portable Document Format) allows anyone with the multi-platform freeware Acrobat Reader to view a wide range of documents incorporating graphics and text with built-in high-quality scalable fonts. As such it is a very popular way of distributing documents online. Word 2007 has an optional add-in that allows you to write your document directly to a PDF file.

Installing the Add-in for PDF

1 Open the Office Button menu, and choose Save As

2 If the option "PDF or XPS" is available then the add-in has already been installed. If it is not there, select the option "Find add-ins for other file formats" instead

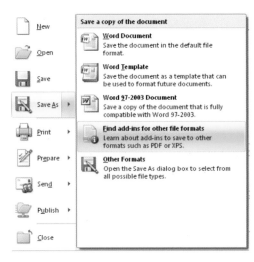

There are many other ways to create PDF files. Adobe itself produces Acrobat writing software, and third parties produce utilities that install special printer drivers into your system. After this you can select the PDF print driver from any application that has a print feature. Instead of printing to paper the driver will generate a PDF file on disk.

3 The Word Help window will appear, explaining how to enable support for export to other file formats. In the "What do you want to do?" section click on the hyperlink "Install and use the Publish as PDF or XPS add-in from Microsoft"

4 This takes you to another help page. Click on the link labeled "Microsoft Save as PDF or XPS Add-in for 2007 Microsoft Office programs". This will take you to your web browser, which will connect to a Microsoft website. Note you will need to be connected to the Internet for this to work

Install and use the Publish as PDF or XPS add-in from Microsoft

To save or export a file to PDF or XPS, you must first install the Publish as PDF or XPS add-in for the 2007 Microsoft Office system.

1. Go to the Microsoft Save as PDF or XPS Add-in for 2007 Microsoft Office programs and follow the instructions on that page.

2. After you install the Publish as PDF or XPS add-in, you can export your file to PDF or XPS. Find links to more information about how to do this in the See Also section.

↑ Top of Page

Install a third-party solution

There may be other solutions available to save or export data from your Microsoft Office program into another format.

1. Visit Microsoft Office Marketplace and browse or search for an add-in.

2. After you obtain the add-in, follow the vendor's instructions on installing and using the add-in.

NOTE The third-party products discussed in this article are manufactured by vendors independent of Microsoft. Microsoft makes no warranty, implied or otherwise, regarding the performance or reliability of these products.

Don't forget

Other Add-ins are available for Word – the process to install these is similar to the example in this chapter.

2007 Microsoft Office Add-in: Microsoft Save as PDF or XPS ☆

Brief Description
This download allows you to export and save to the PDF and XPS formats in eight 2007 Microsoft Office programs. It also allows you to send as e-mail attachment in the PDF and XPS formats in a subset of these programs.

On This Page
↓ Quick Details   ↓ Overview
↓ System Requirements   ↓ Instructions
↓ Related Resources

Continue   Validation Recommended

This download is available to customers running genuine Microsoft Office. Please click the Continue button to begin Office validation. As described in our privacy statement, Microsoft will not use the information collected during validation to identify or contact you.

83

5 Click the Continue button. Depending on the current policy, you may then be asked to validate your Office installation. Select Yes, and then click Continue

Validate Office and obtain the download
◉ Yes, please validate Office and take me to the download. (If an ActiveX dialog box appears, please click **Yes**.)
◯ No, do not validate Office at this time, but take me to the download.

Continue

6 If the Internet Explorer Security Warning dialog appears, click the Install button

7 The web page will show you summary details of the file you are about to download, including estimated download times. If you are happy with this click the Download button

...cont'd

8 The File Download dialog will now appear. Click on the Run button, unless you want to save the file so that you can install it later, or copy it to a computer that is not online

9 If you clicked Save then the above dialog will appear. Use the normal Windows controls to navigate to the desired folder and then click Save

10 When the Download Complete dialog appears click Run

11 Another Security Warning dialog may appear at this point. If so then click Run once again

12 The next dialog informs you that Windows is now configuring the Save as PDF or XPS add-in

Beware

Do not click Cancel at this point or you will have to go all the way back to step 1.

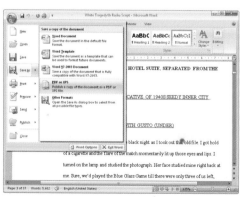

You have now successfully installed the add-in. The "Find add-ins for other file formats" option in the Save As submenu has now been replaced with "PDF or XPS".

Exporting to PDF

You are now ready to create the document. Now that the add-in is installed, saving to PDF is very easy.

1 Open the Office Button menu, choose Save As and then "PDF or XPS". The following dialog appears:

Hot tip

Click the Options... button to see export options such as the facility to create bookmarks automatically from your document headings.

2 Make sure PDF is selected for "Save as type". Enter the filename or leave it at its default, which is the same as the document name but with type PDF

The created document can now be opened and read within Adobe Acrobat Reader:

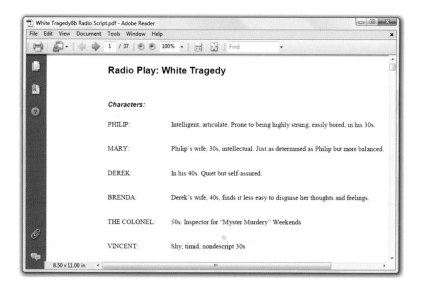

Hot tip

If you don't have the Acrobat Reader on your PC it can be downloaded free of charge from the site www.adobe.com

Exporting to XPS

XPS (XML Paper Specification) is another format that can be used for publishing documents online. XPS files can be viewed directly in Internet Explorer, without the need for a separate reader program.

The add-in you installed in the previous example supports XPS as well as PDF.

1 Open the Office Button menu, choose Save As and select "PDF or XPS"

2 In the option "Save as Type" select XPS Document

3 Close Word and then locate the new file. If you double-click on it, it will automatically display in the browser:

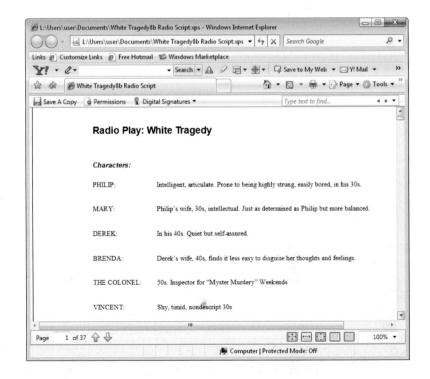

White Tragedy8b Radio Script
Microsoft Office Word Docu...
42.8 KB

White Tragedy8b Radio Script
Adobe Acrobat 7.0 Document
291 KB

White Tragedy8b Radio Script
XPS document
477 KB

6 The Insert Tab

This chapter looks at the different controls available in the Insert Command Tab. It covers building blocks and working with graphics, pages, tables, hyperlinks, headers and footers, as well as some interesting effects that can be applied to text.

Using Building Blocks

Building blocks are components that can be used in many documents. You can define your own building blocks, or download more from Microsoft.

Downloading a Building Block

1 Open or create a Word document. Activate the Insert Command Tab

2 In the Text area, click on the Quick Parts control to access its pop-up menu. Select "Get More on Office Online", making sure you first have an active Internet connection

3 Your browser will display pages from Microsoft Office Online with a range of building blocks available

4 If you find a block you want to use, click the Download button. Once downloading is complete you will see something similar to the following screen:

Where is my new building block?

You have just downloaded a new building block to use in Microsoft® Office Word 2007.

To use your new building block:

1. If you have Word 2007 open, close and then restart Word.
2. On the **Insert** tab, click **Cover Page**, **Header**, **Footer**, **Page Number**, or **Equation**, depending on the type of building block you downloaded.
3. In the gallery you opened, under **From Office Online**, click the new building block to insert it into your document.

Was this information helpful?

[Yes] [No] [I don't know]

Do not worry if what you see does not exactly match this example – websites, including Microsoft's, are continually being revised and updated.

Don't forget

Quitting and restarting Word is necessary so that the new building block can be initialized and then made available.

5 Repeat this process to download more building blocks if required. When you are done, quit and restart Word

6 In the Text area of the Insert Tab click on Quick Parts and select Building Blocks Organizer. You will be able to see all available building blocks, including those that you just downloaded

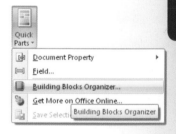

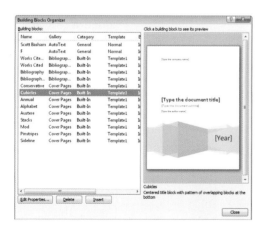

Have a look at the Gallery column in this dialog. "Cubicles", which is selected, is in the gallery "Cover Pages". This means that you can also insert it by going to the Pages area of the Insert Tab and clicking on the Cover Page control. This will call up the Cover Page gallery.

89

...cont'd

Adding a Cover Page

As we saw in the last example, a cover page is a special type of building block that is part of the Cover Pages Gallery.

1 Click on the Cover Page icon in the Pages area of the Insert Tab

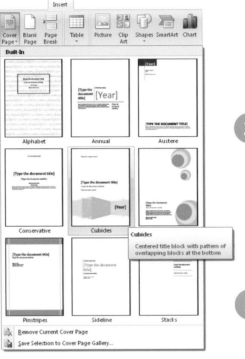

2 Select the desired cover page from the gallery that appears

3 The cover page is automatically added to the start of your document

4 Edit the document by overtyping the fields [Company], [Title], [Subtitle], [Author] and [Year]. The formatting work has already been done for you

Hot tip

When you see text in the form "[Type in here]" this usually indicates the presence of a text field. If you click directly on one of these fields the display will change to something similar to the illustration below. You can now edit the text contents, and Word will preserve all the other attributes.

Creating your own Building Blocks

You can select any text or other objects within Word and make these into new building blocks.

1 Create your content for your new building block. In this example we've created and formatted some standard text that could be reused in several documents

2 Select your content; then go to the Text area of the Insert Tab, click Quick Parts and select "Save Selection to Quick Parts Gallery"

Quick Parts are useful if you need to use standard formatted text across many documents. An example may be a disclaimer that has been agreed with the legal department of your company – it may be company policy to include this in any correspondence with customers.

91

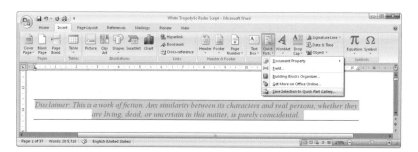

3 The Create New Building Block dialog appears. Enter a name and select a Gallery to use (in most cases this should be the Quick Parts Gallery)

4 Choose a Category and enter a text description

5 Next to "Save in" choose the Word template that will store the building block. If you select "Normal" then the building block will be available to all documents

6 The Options available are "Insert content only", "Insert content in its own paragraph" and "Insert content in its own page". Choose the appropriate option and then click OK. Your building block is now installed and ready for use

...cont'd

Using your own Building Blocks

Once you have created your own building blocks you can use them in the same way as the others.

1 Navigate to the part of your document where you want to add your building block and click an insertion point

2 Click the Quick Parts button and select your building block from its gallery. It will be added at the current position

Editing an Existing Building Block

If you have an example of a building block somewhere in your document, then you can edit this and reattach it to the gallery.

1 Make the necessary changes to the content; then select it

2 Click on Quick Parts and choose "Save Selection to Quick Part Gallery"

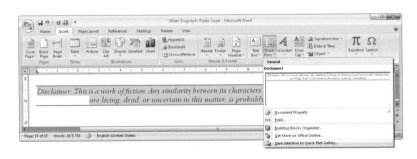

3 If you enter the same name and Gallery as before then the original building block's definition will be overwritten

Don't forget

To replace an existing building block, you must enter precisely the same name in the Create New Building Block dialog.

Adding Pages

The Pages area of the Insert Command Tab has three controls for working with pages. You've already seen Cover Page in the previous building blocks example.

Adding New Pages

Normally you don't need to do anything to add pages to your document – as you add text and other objects Word automatically makes room for them by creating new pages as necessary.

1 Click the Blank Page icon to add a new blank page at your current position

Adding a Page Break

1 Click the Page Break icon. Everything after the current cursor position will move to the next page

Navigating by Page

1 Go to the Home Command Tab, locate the Editing area and click the Find icon

2 Move to the Go To tab, enter the desired page number and click Go To

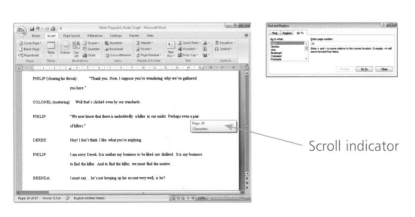

Scroll indicator

3 You can also drag the vertical scroll box, watching the scroll indicator until it displays the page you want

Hot tip

When you are entering text you can type Ctrl+Return to force Word to move to the next page.

Don't forget

If you accidentally create the page break in the wrong place simply click the Undo icon or type Ctrl+Z.

Hot tip

A shortcut for both steps 1 and 2 is to type Ctrl+G. This will open the Go To tab in the relevant dialog.

Pictures

The Illustrations area

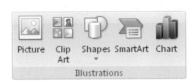

The Illustrations area of the Insert Tab allows you to add a range of different graphical objects.

94

Adding a Picture from a File on Disk

In this example we'll import an image created by a digital camera.

1 Navigate to the appropriate part of your document; then click on Picture in the Illustrations area of the Insert Tab

The search feature (top right corner) works in the same way as it does in the dialog you use for opening Word files.

2 If you move your mouse over one of the images you'll see some additional file details

3 If you hold down the mouse on Views (near the top of the dialog) you will be able to adjust the size of the thumbnail images continuously.

4 Once you have found the image you want, select it and then click the Insert button

5 The image is brought into the current page. Note that it has eight round "handles", which can be dragged around if you want to manipulate the image

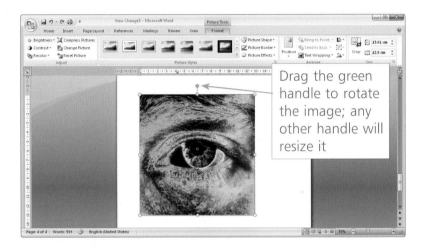

Drag the green handle to rotate the image; any other handle will resize it

Don't forget

Note that the Command Tabs have changed now that we have a picture selected. The Picture Tools Tab is now active – this gives you access to a range of controls for working on your graphic.

95

Editing the Image

Word is not a fully featured graphics package, so extensive editing should be done in a dedicated program that specializes in the particular type of file you are using. There are ways of changing the image within Word, however.

1 To stretch the graphic horizontally drag on either the left or the right handle. Similarly you can stretch the graphic vertically by dragging on either the top or the bottom handle

2 To resize the graphic proportionately drag on any of the corner handles

3 Initially the image behaves as a large single text character – so to move it you need to adjust attributes such as left indent. To move it freely right-click on it, choose Text Wrapping and select an option other than "In Line with Text". You will now be able to move it simply by dragging

...cont'd

4 Sometimes you may wish to use only part of an image. Cutting away the parts you don't need is called cropping. To do this click the Crop icon in the Size area of the Format tab. The handles change into black lines. If you drag these inwards only part of the image will remain

5 There are many other Picture Tools. In this example we have opened the gallery of Picture Shapes and selected one called "Explosion 2". The shape is used to crop the image in a non-rectangular way

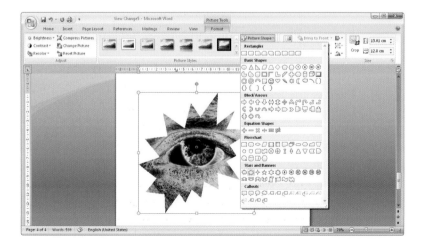

Adding a Draw-Type Picture From a File on Disk

In this example we'll import and manipulate a draw-type object.

1 Navigate to the appropriate part of your document; then click on Picture in the Illustrations area of the Insert Tab

2 Once you've found a suitable draw-type graphic select it and then click the Insert button

Don't forget

Draw-type graphics can generally be edited with no appreciable loss in quality, as they are stored as a set of mathematical objects.

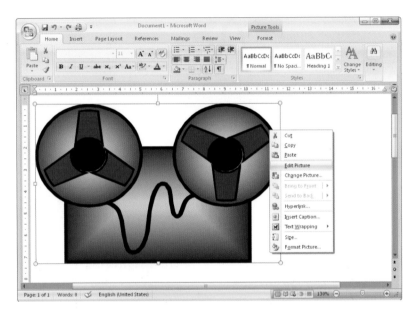

3 If the graphic consists of a number of shapes, then it is usually possible to edit its individual components. To do this right-click and choose Edit Picture

4 Often this will be sufficient for you to start editing individual elements. Experiment by clicking on different areas of the graphic to see what you can select. Once an element is selected it can usually be moved, resized, rotated or formatted using color or line styles

5 Sometimes a draw-type graphic consists of items that are grouped together. If it does you can break it down further by right-clicking and choosing Grouping and then Ungroup

...cont'd

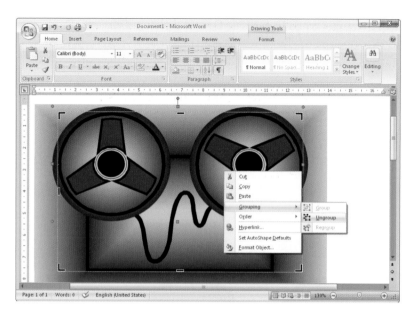

Beware

Paint-type graphics cannot be manipulated in this way. They are represented as a grid of rectangular pixels (picture cells) rather than mathematical objects. This means they cannot be broken down into simpler objects.

6 The graphic is now split into a set of smaller objects

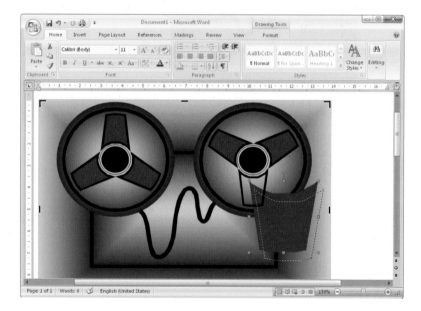

7 Experiment by editing one or two objects; then right-click and choose Grouping and then Regroup. The graphic will behave as a single item once more

Clip Art

Clip art refers to collections of standard images available for use in your document. These are usually organized in some way so that you can easily search for a particular symbol or image.

1 Click the Clip Art icon in the Illustrations area of the Insert Tab. A set of Clip Art controls appears at the right-hand edge of the screen

2 Enter some text in the "Search for" area, open the menu next to "Search in" and choose where to search. You may see this dialog:

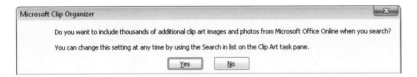

3 Make sure you are connected to the Internet and then click Yes. There will be a delay while Word searches the online content

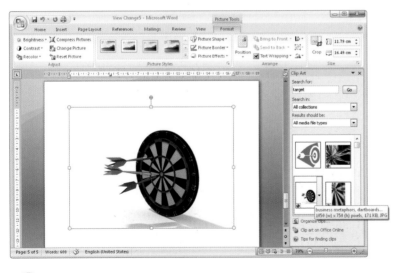

Hot tip

When you click on the image in the Clip Art results list you also have the option Make Available Offline. This will copy the file to your PC so that you can access it even when you are not connected to the Internet.

4 Browse through the results. If you can't find anything suitable then try using different search text. If you find an image you like, click on it and select Insert. It will appear at the current insertion point

Shapes

Word offers a large selection of standard graphic shapes that can be drawn and then customized.

1 Click on the Shapes icon in the Insert Command Tab. A gallery of standard shapes appears

2 Select one of these. This example uses Down Arrow Callout

3 Now click and drag diagonally on the page to create the initial shape. Do not worry if it's the wrong size or position, as both of these can be changed easily

Don't forget

Since Shapes are draw-type graphics you can resize and manipulate them in other ways without any loss in quality.

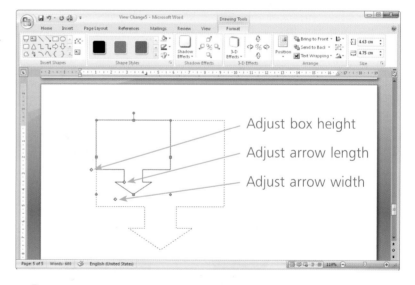

Adjust box height

Adjust arrow length

Adjust arrow width

4 You can move the object by dragging directly on it. Drag on a blue square or circular handle to resize it

5 Drag on a yellow diamond-shaped handle to change a single aspect of the shape. Precisely what this changes depends on the shape you drew, so it is worth experimenting to see what you can do in each case

Text Wrap

Text wrap allows you to define how your graphic interacts with any nearby text. As you saw in the section on Pictures, the default of "In Line with Text" means that the image is treated as a large text character. Sometimes this is useful, but often you need more flexibility in how you position an image.

1 Select your graphic and click on Text Wrapping in the Arrange section of the Format Command Tab

2 If you select Square, Tight or "Top and Bottom" then Word will apply a boundary to your object, and nearby text will keep outside that boundary

3 Next, if you choose Edit Wrap Points from the same pop-up menu you will be able to edit the text wrap border. Simply drag one of the black dot "handles" to move the boundary line. Clicking and dragging on the border, but not on an existing handle, will create a new handle. Using these controls you can alter the way text flows around any irregular shape

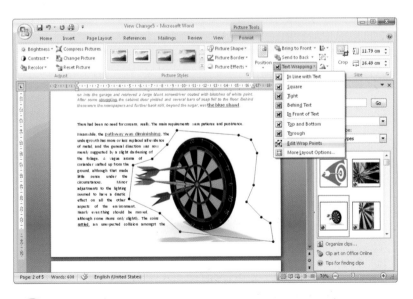

Hot tip

To delete a text wrap handle hold down the Ctrl key and click directly on the handle.

4 For access to controls to help with automatic text wrap choose More Layout Options from the same menu

...cont'd

Applying Styles and Effects to Shapes

1 Make sure your shape is selected. Click on Shadow Effects in the Format Tab and choose one of the perspective shadow effects

In the menu attached to the Shapes tool there is an additional option to create a New Drawing Canvas. This lets you click and drag a rectangular area on the page. Within this area you can add elements such as pictures, clip art and shapes without worrying about text wrap. The canvas behaves as if it were a single graphic item, so you can specify Text Wrap attributes if you so desire.

102

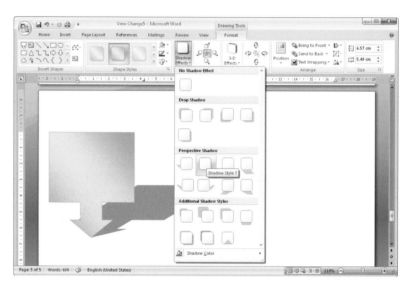

2 You can also add text within a shape. Making sure your shape is still selected click on the Edit Text icon in the Insert Shapes area of the Format Tab

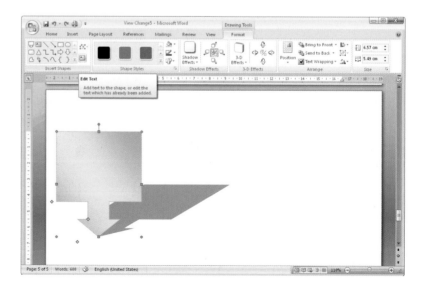

3 An insertion point appears inside the shape. Enter your text and format it using the techniques you learned in Chapter 3

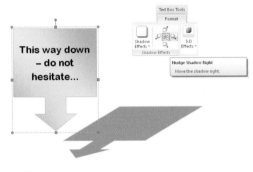

4 You can also customize effects that you've already applied, for example by using the Nudge Shadow controls, which are part of the Shadow Effects area of the Tab. Click on the up, left, right or down nudge icons to move the shadow around

5 Experiment with these controls on other graphic items

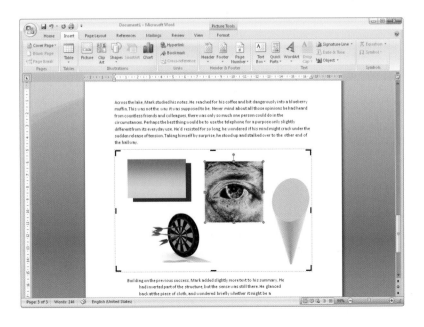

SmartArt

SmartArt graphic items allow you to present concepts and information in a visual way.

 Click on the SmartArt icon in the Insert Tab. The following dialog appears. Choose an item and click OK

When a SmartArt object is selected a new Command Tab appears named SmartArt Tools. You can use this to change colors, switch layouts or apply different styles. In this example some more interesting shaded fills were selected.

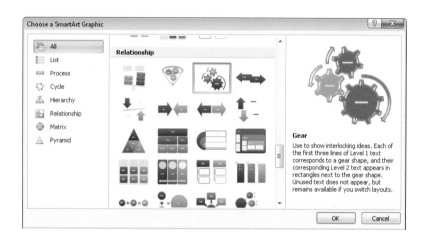

 Enter your text in the window on the left, and it will appear in the diagram. If you right-click anywhere within the object you can choose to add a caption

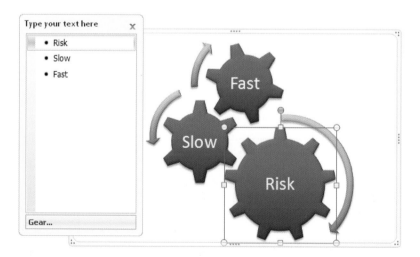

FIGURE 1 – this is a SmartArt concept

 You can customize parts of the object if you click on them

Charts

If you have used Microsoft Excel, you may be familiar with the concept of presenting tables of figures in chart form.

1 Click on the Chart icon in the Insert Tab. The following dialog appears, with a large selection of chart variants:

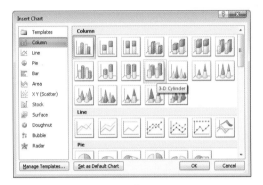

2 Choose a chart type and click OK

3 A default chart appears. You can select and customize this using the Chart Tools Tab, which appears automatically

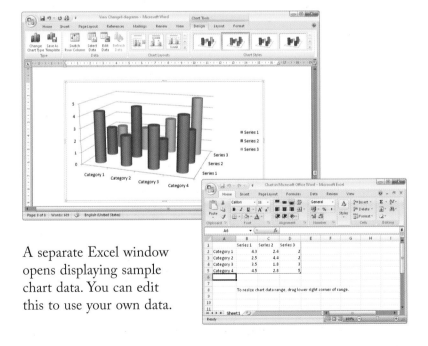

A separate Excel window opens displaying sample chart data. You can edit this to use your own data.

Tables

Tables allow you to organize and manage text in rows and columns. They allow a more visual way of working than you would have with normal text formatted via tab stops.

Inserting a Table

1 Click on the Table icon in the Insert Tab

2 In the grid that appears, click and drag to define an initial table size. Do not worry too much about getting this right first time, as it is easy to change a table's dimensions later on

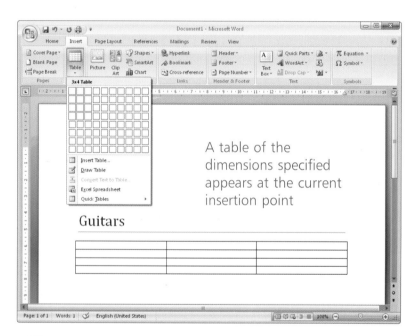

A table of the dimensions specified appears at the current insertion point

3 Alternatively, if you click the Table icon and then choose Insert Table from the submenu, this dialog box appears. You can then specify the table dimensions numerically. Click OK to go ahead and create the table

Resizing a Table

1 Click and drag on the boundary between rows or columns to resize them. Your insertion point will turn into a double-headed arrow as you do this

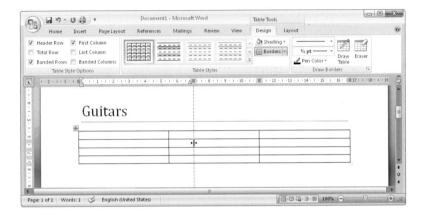

Drawing a Table

You may prefer to use the table drawing tool to create tables. This gives you more flexibility, particularly when you're trying to create irregularly-shaped tables.

1 Click the Table icon and choose Draw Table

2 Click and drag to define the overall table size

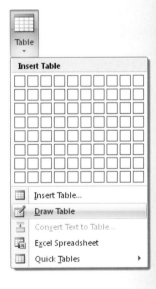

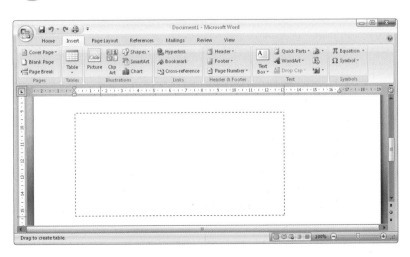

...cont'd

3 Note that the Table Tools command tab is now active, and the Draw Table tool is selected. This means that you can draw onto your new table

4 Click and drag horizontally across the table to draw in the rows. As you drag a dotted line appears, giving you a preview of the new line

Don't forget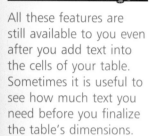

All these features are still available to you even after you add text into the cells of your table. Sometimes it is useful to see how much text you need before you finalize the table's dimensions.

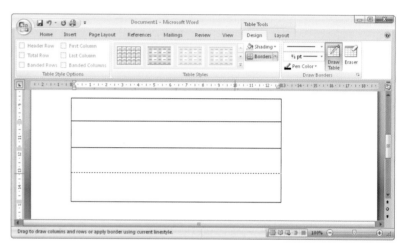

5 Now drag vertically to draw in the column boundaries

6 You can even drag diagonally to create a new line that will divide cells in two, as in the example below

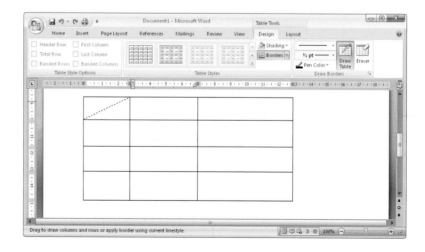

7 Sometimes you will want to remove lines to create an irregular table where some of the cells are much larger. To do this select the Eraser tool and then click directly on the part of the line you wish to remove

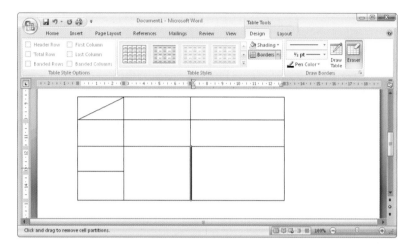

A single click will normally remove the shortest segment at the current mouse position.

If you want to remove larger sections of a line, or even a whole line, then click and drag over the desired area.

8 Once you have erased a fairly large area switch back to the Draw Table tool. You can now add in more lines to this area

9 In the example below you can see how flexible this technique is, allowing for a complex patchwork of odd-sized cells to be created

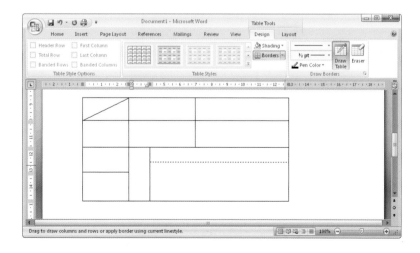

...cont'd

Formatting Your Table

You can use all the formatting techniques learned in earlier chapters on your table text. Often you will start by dragging across an entire row or column to select it prior to formatting.

Guitars

Name	Type	Price
	Semi Acoustic	$1871.00
	Electric	$283.65
Gretsch Duo Jet	Electric	$2853.65

Hot tip

If you have changed the dimensions of individual rows or columns, but now want to make your table more regular again, select the relevant area, right-click and then choose either Distribute Rows Evenly or Distribute Columns Evenly.

Inserting and Deleting Rows or Columns

1 To insert a row, first select an existing row either just above or just below the place where you want the new row

2 Right-click and choose Insert, and then either Insert Rows Above or Insert Rows Below

Guitars

N	Type	Price
Ri	Semi Acoustic	$1871.00
Sq	Electric	$283.65
Gr	Electric	$2853.65

Cut
Copy
Paste
Insert ▸
  Insert Columns to the Left
  Insert Columns to the Right
  Insert Rows Above
  Insert Rows Below
  Insert Cells...
Delete Rows
Merge Cells
Distribute Rows Evenly
Distribute Columns Evenly
Borders and Shading...
Text Direction...
Cell Alignment ▸
AutoFit ▸
Table Properties...

3 The new row will appear in the desired position

4 To insert multiple rows, first click and drag to select the number of rows you wish to add. When you choose Insert Rows Above or Below this number will be added

Merging Cells

Each cell can contain text that is formatted and aligned independently of other cell text (if desired). Sometimes it is useful to group or merge cells together so that they behave as a single cell.

1 Select the cells you wish to merge. Note that these must be next to each other

2 Right-click and choose Merge Cells

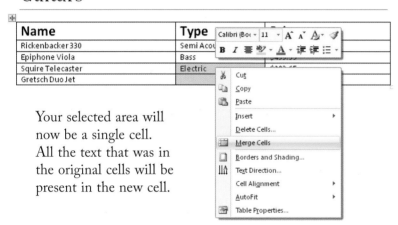

Your selected area will now be a single cell. All the text that was in the original cells will be present in the new cell.

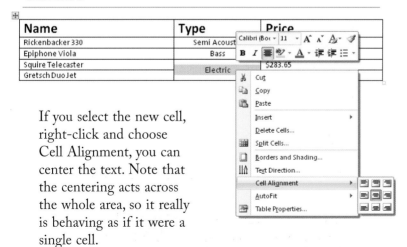

If you select the new cell, right-click and choose Cell Alignment, you can center the text. Note that the centering acts across the whole area, so it really is behaving as if it were a single cell.

...cont'd

Table Properties

 Make sure your insertion point is somewhere inside the table (or select part or all of the table), right-click and then choose Table Properties

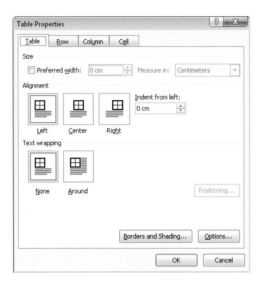

From this dialog you can define properties for the entire table, or at the row, column or cell level.

Table Styles

 Select, or click within, your table and make sure the Table Tools Tab is active. As you hover over each style you will see a preview of your table

 Click on the style to apply it permanently to your table

Hyperlinks and Bookmarks

A hyperlink is usually presented as colored underlined text. Clicking on a hyperlink will normally transport you somewhere else – perhaps to a web page, a different document, or a different position within the current document.

Creating a Hyperlink to a Document on Disk

1 Place your insertion point wherever you want the hyperlink to be added

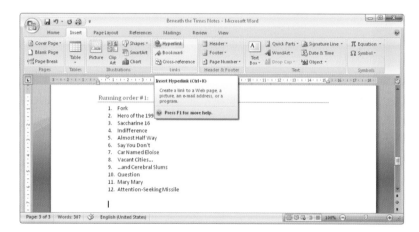

Don't forget

This hyperlinking feature works in much the same way across all Microsoft Office applications.

113

2 In the Links area of the Insert Tab, click Hyperlink – or press Ctrl+K

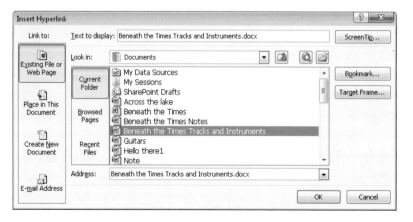

3 For "Link to" choose "Existing File or Web Page" and locate the desired document. Select this and click OK

...cont'd

The hyperlink is inserted into your document. To follow it to its destination hold down the Ctrl key and click the link.

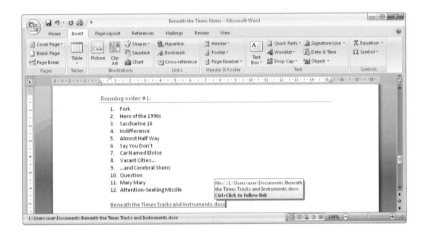

Bookmarks

1 Navigate to the appropriate position in your document. Click on the Bookmark icon in the Links area

Hot tip

You can easily navigate to a bookmark by typing Ctrl+G and selecting Bookmark in the dialog that appears.

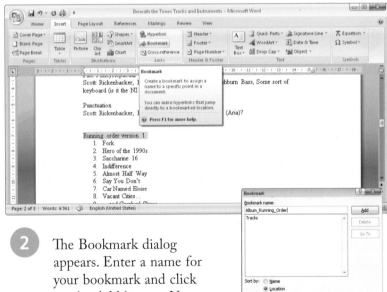

2 The Bookmark dialog appears. Enter a name for your bookmark and click on the Add button. Note that spaces are not allowed in the bookmark name

Headers and Footers

Headers and footers appear at the top and bottom of each page. There are building blocks available with standard designs for these.

Adding a Header or Footer

1 In the Header & Footer area of the Insert Tab click Header or Footer as appropriate

2 Select the design you want. The header or footer will be added to your document

Editing a Header or Footer

1 In the Header & Footer area of the Insert Tab click Header or Footer and then select Edit Header or Edit footer

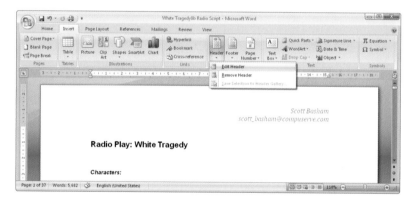

2 You will now be able to edit directly in the Header or Footer area of the page. The Header & Footer Tools Tab appears. From this you can adjust the position of the header and footer, add graphic items, and decide whether headers and footers should be separately defined for odd and even pages (this is useful if your document will be printed double-sided)

3 There is also a Navigation area in the Tab, which allows you to switch between Header and Footer. If your document is divided into sections then Headers and Footers can be defined independently for each section

Hot tip

If there are no header or footer designs in the gallery make sure that building block add-ins are available. To do this select Word Options from the Office Button Menu, and then click Add-Ins. In the Manage list choose Disabled Items and make sure that Building Blocks.dotx is enabled.

...cont'd

Inserting a Date and Time

1 In the Header & Footer Tools Tab, in the Insert area click Date & Time

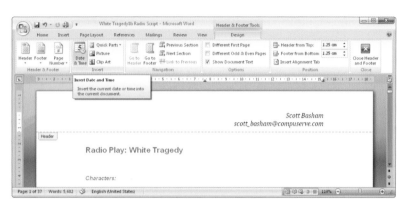

2 Choose from one of the formats listed in the dialog box, and then click OK

3 The current system date and/or time taken from the computer clock are inserted into the current position in your document

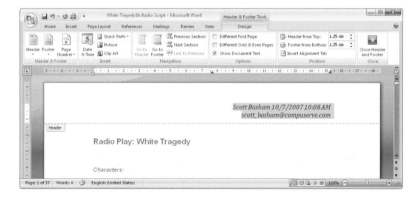

Formatting Page Numbers

Many headers and footers contain automatic page numbers. These can be customized from the Header & Footer area of the Insert tab, or the Header & Footer Tools Tab.

1 Click on the Page Number icon and select Format Page Numbers

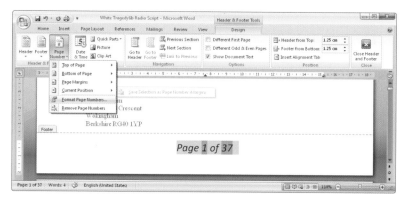

2 The Page Number Format dialog box appears. From this choose a number format

3 If your document is divided into chapters or sections then you can customize the page numbering across these

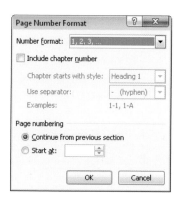

4 You can also force the document or the current section to begin at a certain page. Note that all documents have at least one section by default

Close Header and Footer

1 When you have finished editing click "Close Header and Footer" at the right of the Header & Footer Tools Tab

Hot tip

Another way to shut down Header and Footer editing is simply to double-click in the main page area.

This also works the other way around – if you are editing on the main page you can quickly edit the header or footer simply by double-clicking on either of these.

Advanced Text Effects

WordArt lets you present text using a wide range of visual effects.

Using WordArt

Initially the new WordArt object is inline with the main text, so you can't easily move it by dragging. You can free it by right-clicking, choosing Format WordArt and then selecting a different wrapping style from the Layout tab.

1 Select your text and click WordArt in the Text area of the Insert Tab

2 Choose an effect from the gallery

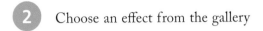

3 Select a font and size, and select bold and/or italic if required

4 Click OK to see the results in your document. You can resize the new object by dragging on its handles

Equations

Creating and Editing an Equation

1 Click an insertion point in the appropriate place. Click on the Equation icon in the Symbols area of the Insert Tab and choose Insert New Equation

2 You can now enter your equation, either by typing directly or by clicking on one of the available symbols

$$\frac{-b \pm \sqrt{b^2 - 4ac}}{2a}$$

3 You can also select one of the pre-built structures. If you can find something similar to what you need then it's much easier to select the structure and edit it rather than entering the whole thing manually

4 Click on the small black arrow to the right of the equation to open the pop-up menu. From here you can change the format to Linear, or even save the equation for later use via the gallery. The illustration below shows the example equation presented as Linear (all on one line)

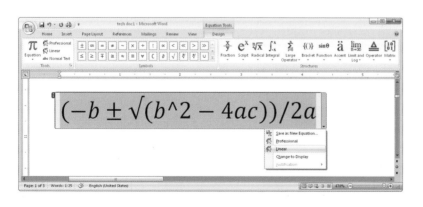

$$(-b \pm \sqrt{(b\text{^}2 - 4ac)})/2a$$

Don't forget

When you are editing an equation a special Equation Tools Command Tab appears. This contains all the controls you need to add or edit equations.

Symbols

Inserting a Symbol

1 Click an insertion point in the appropriate place. Click on the Symbol icon in the Symbols area of the Insert Tab to open the pop-up menu

2 If the symbol you want is in the display of commonly-used items simply click to insert it into your document

3 Otherwise click on More Symbols to access the following dialog box:

From the Symbols page you can choose the Font and Subset to access a wide range of symbols.

4 When you've located the symbol, select it and click Insert

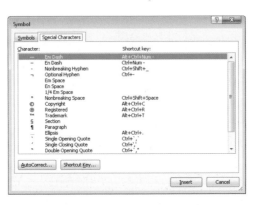

From the Special Characters page you can scroll through a selection of standard special characters. You can also see which of them have keyboard shortcuts.

Hot tip

To assign a keyboard shortcut to a symbol or special character select it from this dialog and then click Shortcut Key.

120

7 The Page Layout Tab

This chapter looks at Themes, and shows you how to organize your document into sections.

Themes

Themes control your overall document design by defining its main colors, fonts and effects. If you use a Theme's colors, for example, then changing theme will change these automatically.

Selecting a Theme

1 Open your document and make the Page Layout Command Tab active

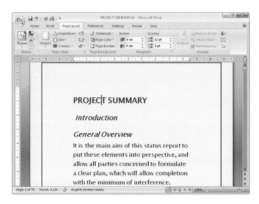

2 Click the Themes button and browse through the Themes in the Gallery. As you hover over an item you will see a preview of the Theme's settings

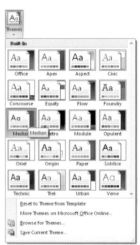

You can also change a Theme's effects independently of its fonts and colors. To do this click on the Effects button in the Themes area and select a different option.

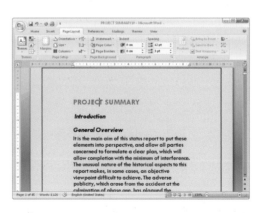

3 Click directly on the Theme to apply it permanently to your document

Colors and Fonts

Working With a Theme's Colors

1 To change just the colors that belong to the Theme, click on the Theme Colors icon in the Themes area. A gallery of color swatches appears

2 Choose a different option. If your document used Theme colors then these will be changed automatically

3 From now on, whenever you select a color you will be able to choose one from the Theme's current selection

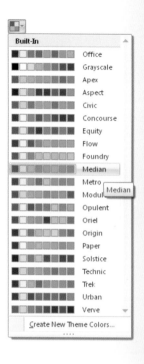

Working With a Theme's Fonts

1 Click on the Fonts icon in the Themes area. A gallery of fonts appears. Each theme contains one font defined for headings, and a second for main body text

2 Choose a different option. If your document used Theme fonts then these will be changed automatically

As you hover over an option, any text currently using Theme fonts will preview the new settings.

3 Now switch back to the Home Command Tab and open the Fonts menu. At the top you will see the two Theme fonts. If you use these then you can easily switch themes later on – and your text will change accordingly

Page Setup

This area of the Page Layout Command Tab contains controls for margins, size and orientation as well as line numbering, adding page and section breaks, and adjusting hyphenation.

Margins

1 Click on the Margins icon to choose from the gallery, or click Custom Margins to define these via a dialog box

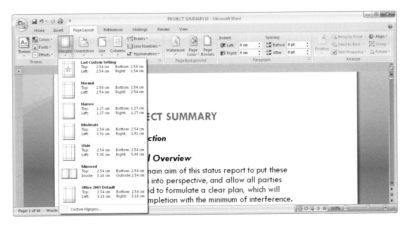

Columns

1 By default your text is set out in a single column spread across the page. To change to a multi-column layout click the Columns icon and choose the number you want. Your text will be reformatted in the new layout

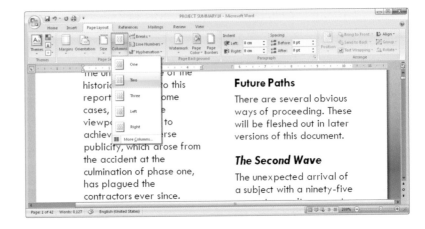

Document Structure

Page Setup Dialog

1 Click on the ▣ icon in the lower right-hand corner of the Page Setup area. The following dialog box appears:

This is divided into three tabbed pages, giving you numeric control of attributes for Margins, Paper and Layout.

You can also access this dialog from some of the icons in the Page Setup area. For example, clicking on Size and choosing More Paper Sizes takes you straight to the Paper page of this dialog.

Hot tip

The Paper tabbed page lets you select the paper size for printed documents. A wide range of preset sizes is available, but if none of these is suitable then you can define your own custom size by entering the dimensions directly.

Dividing your Document into Sections

1 Click on the Breaks button and examine the options within the Section Breaks part of the menu

2 Choose Next Page

...cont'd

The text immediately after the current insertion point is moved to the next page, where your new section begins. Your document now consists of two sections – one before this page break, and a second that runs from this page to the end.

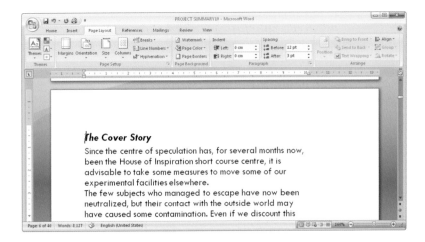

Don't forget

A section need not start on a new page. Choose Breaks, Section Breaks and Continuous to create a new section at the current insertion point. This can be useful if you want to vary the number of columns within a single page.

Sections help to give your document some structure. Many of the layout settings you've seen can apply just to the current section. For example, a section can have its own "local" header & footer and column layout.

Watermarks

 Click on the Watermark button and choose Custom Watermark. Select a picture from the dialog

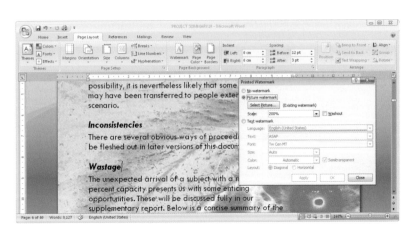

Other Settings

Page Color

1 Click on the Page Color button and choose from the gallery to set the background color of the page

2 To see more options choose More Colors or Fill Effects

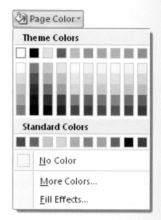

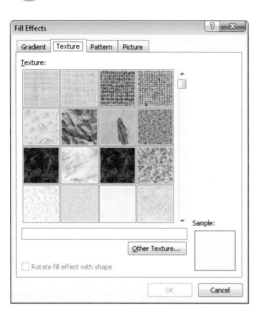

A texture, when chosen, will repeat across the page, filling the whole area. The supplied textures are specifically designed so that you shouldn't be able to see where one "tile" of the texture joins the next.

Hot tip

If you chose a theme for your document then the page color gallery will show you that theme's colors. The main colors are in the top line; in the lines below you will see tonal variations of each of these. Choosing theme colors will give your documents some consistency since these colors are designed to work well together.

The Arrange Tools

1 Select a graphical object and choose Send Behind Text from the Arrange area

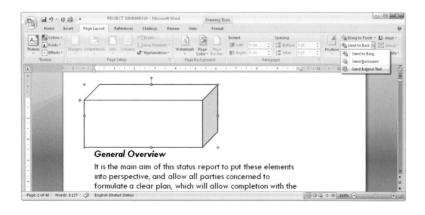

...cont'd

2 The object now appears behind any nearby text. You can now easily reposition it by dragging with the mouse

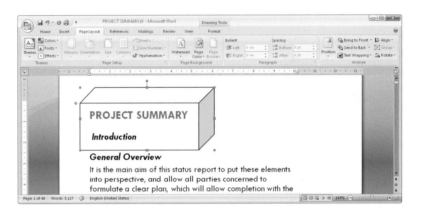

Rotating Objects

1 Select an object

2 In the Arrange area, click on Rotate and choose More Rotation Options. The following dialog appears:

3 Enter a rotation angle and then click OK

Note that this dialog, Format AutoShape, contains many other controls for customizing your selected object.

8 The References Tab

The References Tab helps you work with longer, more formal documents. You will see how to add an index, a table of contents, footnotes, captions, and a bibliography.

Table of Contents

You can automatically create a Table of Contents by asking Word to look for instances of particular styles, or by using entries that you create manually.

Creating a Table of Contents

1 Activate the References Command Tab

2 From the Table of Contents area click Table of Contents and choose "Insert Table of Contents"

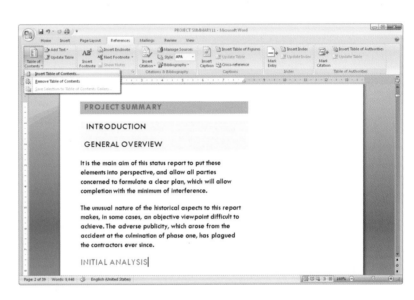

The Table of Contents dialog appears. By default this will build a Table of Contents using the heading styles within your document. You can change the overall look and feel by clicking the Formats pop-up menu.

3 Click OK to build the Table of Contents at the current insertion point. Word calculates the correct page number reference for each entry

Customizing Your Table of Contents

1 If you select an entry in the Table of Contents and activate the Styles window (from the Home Tab) you'll see that it uses a special "TOC..." style

The selected line uses the style TOC 2. All entries at this level use this style.

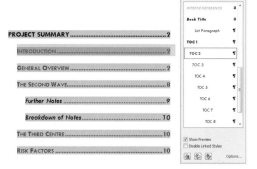

2 If you want to change the formatting of these entries, it is best to change the definition of their styles (see Chapter 3, "Formatting Text") rather than the individual entries themselves. If you format in this way then your changes will be reapplied whenever you rebuild the Table of Contents

Updating Your Table of Contents

1 As you continue to work with your document text may move to different pages, pages may be inserted or deleted, and new headings may be added

2 Click Update Table to rebuild the Table of Contents. You will be given the choice of updating the entire table or just the page numbers of the existing entries

Footnotes

Footnotes allow you to add a superscript number to a piece of text, which relates to explanatory text at the bottom of the page.

Adding a Footnote

 1 Select the desired text and click Insert Footnote or press Ctrl+Alt+F

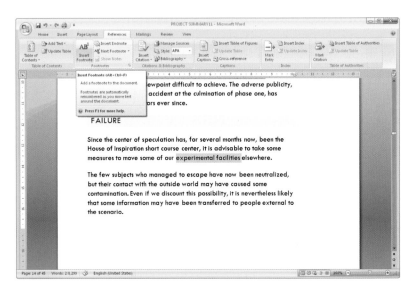

2 Next add the footnote text at the bottom of the page

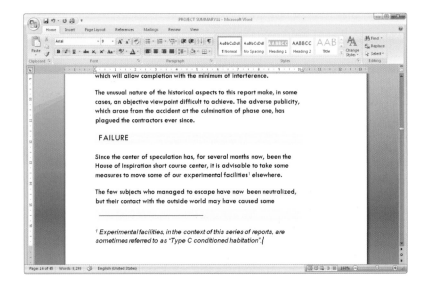

Adding Citations

Citations are useful if you need to add a reference to another author or publication within your text. Later on you can compile a standard bibliography that collects together all your citations.

Adding a Citation

1 Click just after the reference in your main text. Click the Insert Citation button and choose Add New Source

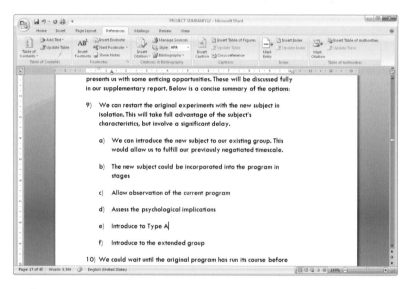

2 The Create Source dialog appears. Enter the details and then click OK

3 A short citation reference now appears next to your text. If you need to change any of the details you entered click the Manage Sources button

> d) Assess the psychological implications
>
> e) Introduce to Type A (Jarce, 1999)
>
> f) Introduce to the extended group

133

Hot tip

If you've already added sources to your document, then you can select one of these from the pop-up menu attached to the Insert Citation button. This allows you to refer to the same source several times without rekeying the details.

Marking Citations

In the previous example you added a citation reference by inserting it into a particular place in your document. This example is slightly different – here you will select some text and mark it as the citation itself.

1 Locate and select the text that you'd like to make into a citation

2 Click the Mark Citation button. (This is in the Table of Authorities area of the References Tab.) The following dialog appears:

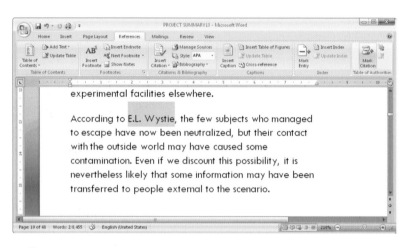

3 Choose a citation Category, or use the Category button to define further categories. Click the Mark button, or Mark All to mark all instances of your text

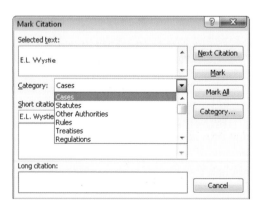

Your text will now be marked as a citation. If you click the Insert Table of Authorities button you will see all the marked entries.

Bibliography

Word can generate bibliographies in a number of formal styles.

Creating a Bibliography

1 Make sure you've inserted citations throughout your document

2 Click on Bibliography and then select from the gallery.

Word will use the sources you previously defined to build the complete bibliography.

You can continue to work with your document, adding more citations and editing the sources using the Manage Sources button.

135

Hot tip

If you've made changes that should be reflected in the bibliography then click anywhere within it. You'll see the following icon, which indicates you've selected a text field:

Click on this to open the field menu, and choose Update Bibliography.

BIBLIOGRAPHY

Jarce, H. (1999). *Group Types Within Isolated Community Experimental Units*. Cambridge: CB and RW Associates.

Pewtey, A. (2001). *A Study in Exasperation - Eightieth Edition*. Purley: APL Press.

Snallrot, E. (2001). *Welding and Corporate Sponsorship*. Manchester: Business Journals Press.

Captions

Adding a Caption to a Graphic Element

1 Select your element

2 Click on Insert Caption in the Captions area

Hot tip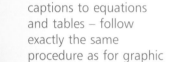

You can also add captions to equations and tables – follow exactly the same procedure as for graphic elements.

3 Add the caption text in the dialog that appears

4 There are three label options – Equation, Figure and Table (you can also use the New Label button to add more options). Choose Figure for this example

5 Choose the Position relative to your selected item. Captions will normally be numbered 1, 2, 3 and so on but this can be changed by clicking on Numbering

Don't forget

As with the footnotes seen earlier, Word automatically renumbers captions as you add to or delete from your document.

6 Click OK when done

Table of Figures

Once you've created captions throughout your document you can ask Word to build a Table of Figures.

1 Make sure your insertion point is placed where you want the Table of Figures

2 Click on Insert Table of Figures

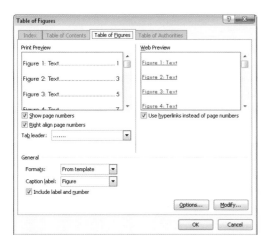

The Table of Figures dialog appears as shown.

3 Choose a format from the pop-up list. The Print and Web Preview areas will show you how this will look

Don't forget

As with footnotes and captions, Word takes care of the numbering and renumbering for you, so you can edit your document without having to worry about reorganizing the Table of Figures.

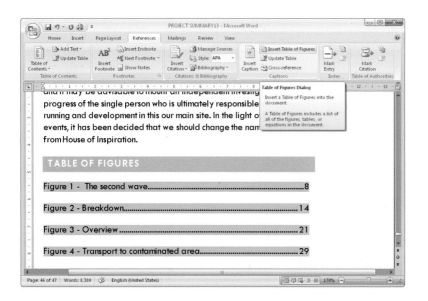

Indexing

Longer documents benefit greatly from a well-organized index. Word makes the process of creating an index fairly easy.

1 Select the text you want to appear in the index, and click on Mark Index Entry or press Shift+Alt+X

2 You can now edit the entry text, add a subentry, and choose whether the index will show the current page, a range of pages or a cross reference to another index entry. When you have made these settings click Mark

If you have the Show/ Hide ¶ option active you will see where your index entries have been marked.

Hot tip

If you edit your document so that the page numbers have changed, or if you have added more index entries, then you will need to rebuild the index. To do this select the index and then click on Update Index.

3 Click Insert Index to see the finished result

9 The Mailings Tab

This chapter examines the features of the Mailings Tab.

Envelopes

Adding Envelopes to your Document

1 Activate the Mailings Command Tab

2 From the Create area click Envelopes. The follow dialog appears:

Hot tip

If you enter a return address you will be shown a dialog asking you whether you want to make this the default return address. If you click Yes then you won't need to retype it the next time you create an envelope.

3 Enter the delivery address and, optionally, the return address. Click on the Options button to select the envelope's dimensions from a list of standard sizes

4 Click Add to Document and your envelope will appear

Labels

Word can create labels using a wide range of standard sizes.

Creating a New Document for your Labels

1 From the Create area click Labels. The follow dialog appears

2 Enter the label text (usually an address) and choose between creating a single label or a full page of many labels

3 Click the Options button and select the label vendor and then the label from the product numbers listed

4 Click OK; then click the New Document

Your labels will be displayed in a new Word document.

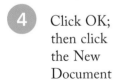

Hot tip

If the label you require isn't listed in the Label Options dialog click the New Label button. This will let you define your own label design by entering all the dimensions numerically.

Mail Merge

There are several ways of setting up mail merging in Word, but the easiest is to use the Wizard, which guides you through the various stages of the process.

Using the Mail Merge Wizard

1 Click on Start Mail Merge and select "Step by Step Mail Merge Wizard"

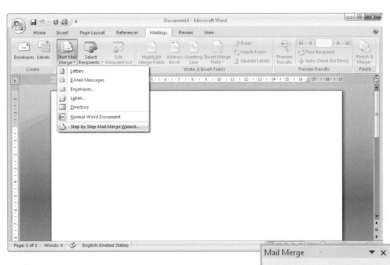

2 The Mail Merge window appears at the right-hand side of the screen. If you drag on its title bar you can make it into a floating window

3 The first step of the process is to choose the document type. In this example we will produce a single letter design, and then print out a copy for each person in a list of addresses. Make sure Letters is selected and then click on the hyperlink "Next: Starting document" at the bottom of the Mail Merge Window

Don't forget

Since setting up Mail Merging involves quite a few steps, it is unlikely to be helpful if you only have one or two recipients planned. If you have a large list of recipients, however, it can be a real time saver.

Mail Merge ▼ ✕

Select document type

What type of document are you working on?

- ◉ Letters
- ○ E-mail messages
- ○ Envelopes
- ○ Labels
- ○ Directory

Letters

Send letters to a group of people. You can personalize the letter that each person receives.

Click Next to continue.

Step 1 of 6

➡ Next: Starting document

Mail Merge ▾ ✕

Select starting document

How do you want to set up your letters?

- ⦿ Use the current document
- ○ Start from a template
- ○ Start from existing document

Use the current document

Start from the document shown here and use the Mail Merge wizard to add recipient information.

Step 2 of 6

➡ Next: Select recipients

⬅ Previous: Select document type

④ At the next step choose "Use the current document" if you are happy to write the letter using the current document. Alternatively you can open a document previously saved or even create a new document based on a template design

⑤ Click the hyperlink "Next: Select recipients" to proceed to the next stage

⑥ There are several ways to define the letter's recipients. If you have previously defined a list then select "Use an existing list". If you use Microsoft Outlook and have created contacts you'd like to use then choose "Select from Outlook contacts". This will allow you to choose which of your Outlook contacts you'd like to use. In this example we will create a new list, so select "Type a new list"

⑦ Click on the "Create" hyperlink

Don't forget

As with all Wizards, the Mail Merge Wizard allows you to move back and forward freely between steps – so you can always go back and change your mind about previous settings.

143

Mail Merge ▾ ✕

Select recipients

- ○ Use an existing list
- ○ Select from Outlook contacts
- ⦿ Type a new list

Type a new list

Type the names and addresses of recipients.

🖳 Create...

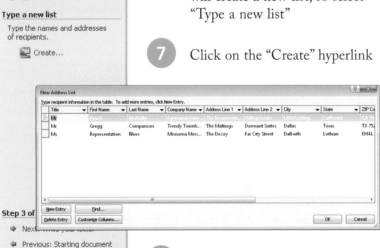

New Address List

Type recipient information in the table. To add more entries, click New Entry.

Title	First Name	Last Name	Company Name	Address Line 1	Address Line 2	City	State	ZIP Co
Mr	Peach	McNulty	Egmaaua Enter...	The Inconvenie...	Hilltop Estate	Jollyfretting	California	CA 94
Mr	Gregg	Comparison	Trendy Townh...	The Maltings	Dormant Suites	Dallas	Texas	TX 752
Ms	Representation	Blues	Misnoma Merc...	The Decoy	Far City Street	Dalkeith	Lothian	EH4L

New Entry   Find...

Delete Entry   Customize Columns...   OK   Cancel

Step 3 of

➡ Next: ~~Write your letter~~

⬅ Previous: Starting document

⑧ Enter the details of each recipient and then click OK

...cont'd

9 The next dialog asks you to save your list to disk. This is useful because you may wish to use the list again in the future. Enter a file name and click Save

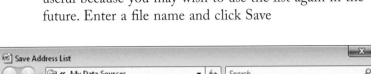
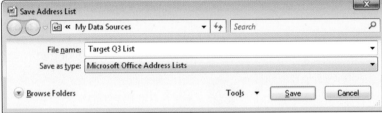

10 In the MailMerge Recipients dialog make sure all of the lines are selected

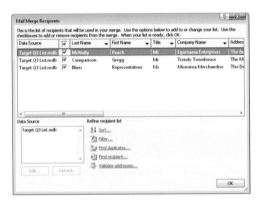

If your data source was a previously-saved list, or your Outlook contacts, then you might decide to select some rather than all the items.

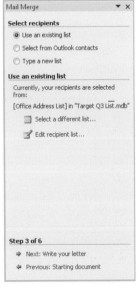

11 Click OK. Back in the main screen the Mail Merge window now displays a summary of the recipients selected

12 From this page of the wizard you can edit the recipient list, or even select a different list altogether

13 When you are happy with your choice of recipients click the hyperlink marked "Next: Write your letter"

14 You can now start working on your letter, typing in and formatting text as usual. In addition to this, you will want to add one or more special Mail Merge fields

15 Place your insertion point where you'd like the address and click the Address Block icon in the Write & Insert Fields area of the Mailings Command Tab

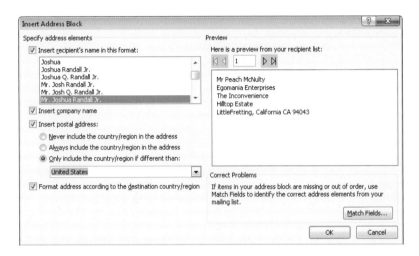

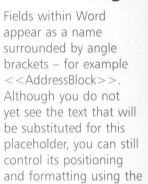

Don't forget

Fields within Word appear as a name surrounded by angle brackets – for example <<AddressBlock>>. Although you do not yet see the text that will be substituted for this placeholder, you can still control its positioning and formatting using the normal editing controls.

16 Choose a format style, checking the preview area to see the effect of different choices. When you click OK you'll see the placeholder <<AddressBlock>> appear

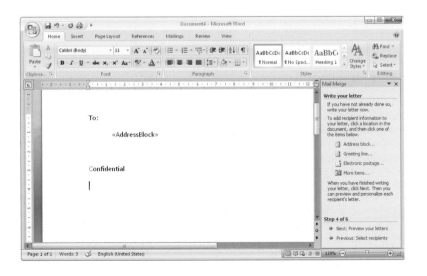

...cont'd

17 You can also add an automatic Greeting Line near the top of your letter. Word will substitute in each name and salutation when the document is printed. Place your insertion point in the correct place and then click Greeting Line. The following dialog appears:

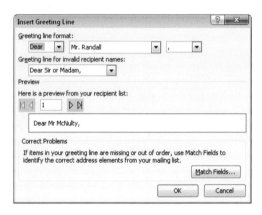

18 Choose the appropriate format and click OK

19 Click on Preview Results to see how your letters will print. Finally complete the merge by clicking on Print in the Mail Merge window

Hot tip

When previewing the Mail Merge results you can move to each recipient to check that each instance of your letter looks OK. The controls for moving back and forth are in the Preview Results area of the Mailings tab, and also on the fifth page of the Mail Merge Wizard screen as shown here.

10 The Review Tab

The Review Tab gives you various ways of checking your work, as well as tracking changes that may need to be reviewed by you or others.

Spelling and Grammar Check

Word has access to a number of English and non-English dictionaries, which it uses when running spelling checks.

Checking Selected Text

1 Select the text you want to check

2 Make sure the Review Command Tab is active. Click on the Spelling & Grammar icon in the Proofing area

Once the check is completed you will be asked whether you want to check the rest of the document.

3 If Word detects any errors in your text, you will see the Spelling and Grammar dialog box

Word will show you suggestions for spelling corrections – select one and click on Change or Change All. If the word was correct but not in Word's dictionary you can click on the "Add to Dictionary" button.

In this example the spelling checker has found a word which, while spelled correctly, may be an incorrect choice (based on the surrounding text). In this case it correctly suggests the replacement word.

Hot tip

To run a spelling check on the entire document, make sure that no text at all is selected when you click the Spelling & Grammar icon.

Don't forget

In this example the dictionary language is English (United States). Language is one of the editable attributes of a Text Style – so you may want to define particular styles to use particular languages. See Chapter 3, "Formatting text", for more information on working with styles.

If the "Check grammar" checkbox is selected Word will apply a set of grammar rules to your text. In this example the rule "Subject-Verb Agreement" was violated.

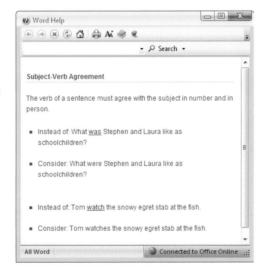

If Word comes up with multiple suggestions for correcting your grammar, it will list them with the word OR between each item and the next. If one of these suggestions is acceptable to you, select the item and then click the Change button.

4 If Word finds a possible grammatical error you can either accept one of its suggestions by clicking the Change button or ignore the recommendation (click Ignore Once, or Ignore Rule if you don't want Word to apply this rule in future).

If you click the Explain button Word's Help window appears with a description of the current rule.

When you have finished reading, close this window.

5 If you want to stop the spelling and grammar check before it's finished click the Close button, or manually close the dialog window by clicking the "x" icon in its top right corner

6 From within the Spelling and Grammar dialog click on Options to review or customize the way the check runs

...cont'd

The following dialog box appears.

You can also access this dialog from the Office Button menu – click the Word Options button and then choose Proofing.

This gives you access to a range of settings, grouped separately into spelling and grammar sections.

The Custom Dictionaries button lets you access the list of words you've added when running the spelling check.

7 Under the "When correcting spelling and grammar in Word" heading, click Settings

8 The Grammar Settings dialog contains three sets of options. "Require" is for general punctuation and spacing rules. "Grammar" is a list of groups of grammatical rules. "Style" is a list of less strict rules – breaking these is more a matter of taste, and will probably depend on how formal the current document is

9 Click OK to this and to the Word Options dialog to return to the spelling and grammar checker

10 When Word has finished checking your document you will see a confirmation dialog

Thesaurus

1 Select a single word and then click on the Thesaurus icon in the Proofing tab

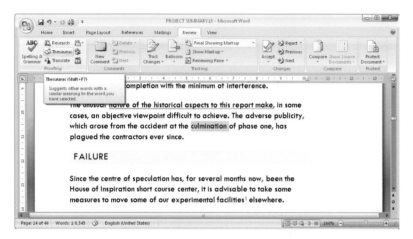

Don't forget

A Thesaurus is a collection of synonyms (words with identical or similar meanings).

2 The Research pane appears – this can be moved or resized simply by dragging with the mouse. It contains a list of words that have a similar meaning to that of the one you selected

3 Select one of the options

4 From the pop-up menu that appears you can choose to insert the selected item, or copy it to the clipboard

5 Alternatively select Look Up to search the Thesaurus again, this time with the new selected word

Translation

There are a number of built-in bilingual dictionaries, which allow you to see translations of words or sentences.

Translating Selected Text

1 Select one or more words and then click on the Translate icon in the Proofing area

2 In the Research Pane choose English in the From field, and the desired target language in the To field

Don't forget

As well as a definition of the word selected, the dictionary also gives you an indication of pronunciation using standard phonetics.

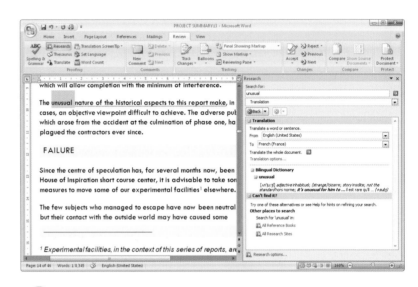

3 The translated text appears in the lower half of the Research Pane

Translating the Whole Document

1 Make sure the Research Pane is visible – if not then click on the Translate icon in the Proofing area

2 Click the arrow next to "Translate the whole document"

3 Click Yes when the confirmation message appears. You will be taken to the WorldLingo website, where you will be able to see part of your document translated free of charge. To convert large amounts of text at a professional level you will need to ask for a quote. Instructions on how to do this are available at the website

Beware

Because the Translate Whole Document feature uses a remote translation service, you need to be connected to the Internet for this feature to work.

Using ScreenTips for Translation

This feature allows you quickly to see a translation for a small piece of text.

1 Select the text you wish to translate; then right-click

2 Choose Translate and then the language you want to see

3 From now on, whenever you leave your pointer over a word for a few moments, a ScreenTip will appear with its translation

The unusual nature of the historical a̲s̲~~~~ke, in some cases, an objective viewpoint difficult ~~~~se publicity, which arose from the accident at the culmination of phase one, has plagued the contractors ever since.

culmination
[kʌlmɪˈneɪˌʃn] apogée *féminin*

Research

Word provides a range of options for looking up reference information based on text you select.

Using an Encyclopedia

1 Select the relevant text and then click the Research button

2 In the Research Pane the "Search for" field should contain your selected text. In the field below this open the pop-up menu and choose a reference book or site. In this example the Encarta Encyclopedia has been used to provide information about a city in Africa

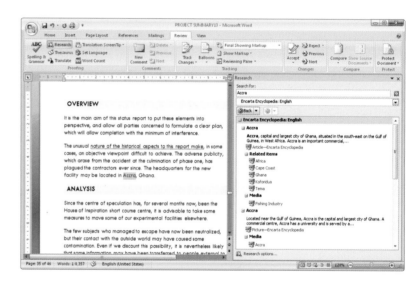

Hot tip

If you click on "Research options..." at the bottom of the Research Pane, the dialog illustrated below appears.

This lets you control which services and sites are used for research.

You can use the hyperlinks in the main area of the Research Pane to access articles from Encarta or other related sources.

Comments

Adding a Comment

① Select the text

② Click the New Comment icon in the Comments area

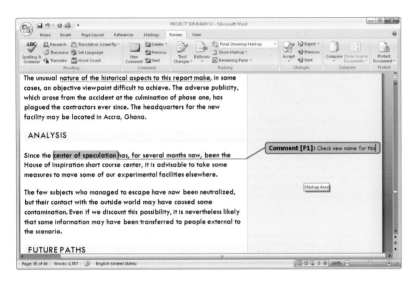

155

Hot tip

Comments are automatically renumbered as you add and delete them from your document.

③ Add the comment text in the Markup Area at the right

④ Repeat this process to add more comments

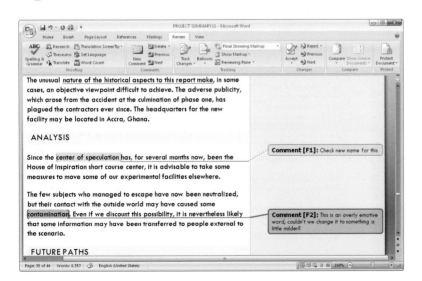

Hot tip

If you allow your mouse to rest over a commented piece of text the comment will appear as a ToolTip. This is useful if you cannot see the Markup Area (if you are working in Draft mode, for example).

Tracking Changes

Sometimes it is useful to track changes you make to a document, so that someone else can see exactly what you have done. It may even be necessary for someone to approve or reject those changes before they become permanently incorporated into the document.

1 To activate change tracking, click the Track Changes icon in the Tracking area

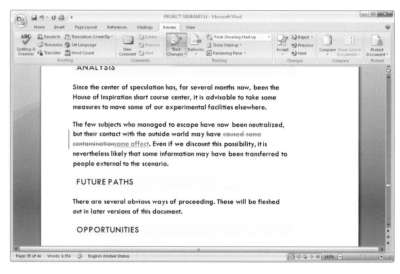

2 Now your edits will be shown visually

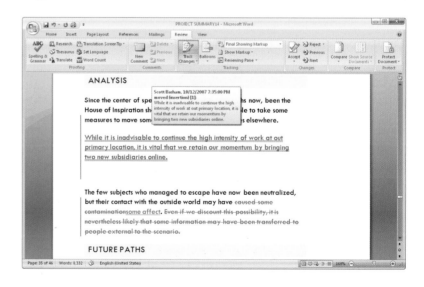

3 Click on the Balloons icon in the Tracking area, and choose "Show Revisions in Balloons" to see all the revision details in the Markup area

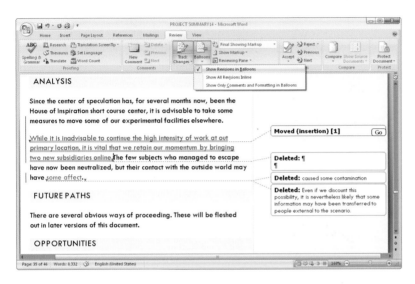

4 Click on the Reviewing Pane icon in the Tracking area, and choose one of the two options to make it visible

The Reviewing Pane contains a comprehensive summary of all the revisions made, plus all the added comments.

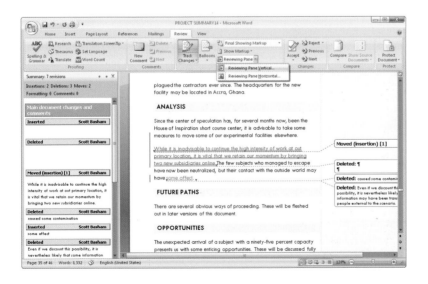

Hot tip

The Tracking tools also allow you to change the way your document is displayed. You can show the final or the original version, with and without the changes marked up.

You can also customize which types of changes will be displayed as markup.

Accepting and Rejecting

Now there are some changes in your document you can take on the role of someone who reviews these changes. The tools in the Changes area let you work through your document looking at each change in turn – using the Previous and Next icons.

If you click the Accept button then the change is permanently applied to the document.

If you click Reject instead, the change is removed and the text reverts to its original state.

Comparing Documents

Word allows you to divide the screen into a number of panes so that you can quickly see the differences between versions of the same basic document.

1 Click on the Compare tool in the Compare area, and choose the first option

2 The following dialog appears. Choose two documents to compare and then click OK

3 If either of the documents contains tracked changes then the following dialog will appear. Click Yes

4 The screen will now divide into panes that depict the two source documents (at the right-hand side in this example), with a third larger pane that illustrates the comparison between the two

5 As before, the Reviewing Pane lists changes – this time it's the changes between the two documents. Word regards the first document you specified as the "original". It scans through the second document, and registers any differences it finds as revisions to be listed

6 Use the tools in the Changes area to move between changes, and click the Accept or Reject button, either to apply the second document's revisions or to revert to the state of play in the original document

7 If you do not need to see the source documents then click the Show Source Documents icon and choose Hide Source Documents

8 As part of this process you have created a new document called "Compare Result" with a numeric suffix. If you are happy with the accept and reject decisions you made then save this document under a different name

Hot tip

You can also use the Show Source Documents icon to show just one of the source documents, as well as to show both or to show neither.

Protecting a Document

Word allows you to protect your document in a number of ways. You can control which aspects may be edited – for example, you may allow a user to add comments but not to edit the text directly.

1 Click the Protect Document icon and choose the option "Restrict Formatting and Editing". The Restrict Formatting and Editing window appears

2 Activate the option to "Limit formatting to a selection of styles" and click the Settings hyperlink. The Formatting Restrictions dialog appears

3 Choose the styles that are to be allowed in your document and click OK

4 When you are happy with your settings click the "Yes, Start Enforcing Protection" button at the bottom of the Restrict Formatting and Editing window. You are then prompted to enter a password, which can be used to unlock the document for full editing later on

5 The window now indicates that the document is restricted, with a summary of the current restrictions that apply

Hot tip

In section 2 of the Restrict Formatting and Editing window you can set restrictions to allow only tracked changes, comments or fields within forms to be entered by the user.

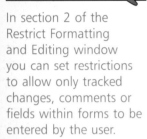

Don't forget

Once the document is protected you will need to remember your password if you want to unlock it for full editing. To unlock it click the Stop Protection button and then enter the password.

11 The View Tab

The View Tab gives you a selection of controls for looking at your document in different ways.

Document Views

Full Screen Reading View

1 Make sure the View Command Tab is active. In the Document Views area click the Full Screen Reading icon

Hot tip

Word 2007 uses two new fonts, Calibri (for body text) and Cambria (for headings), which are specially designed for easy reading on a computer screen.

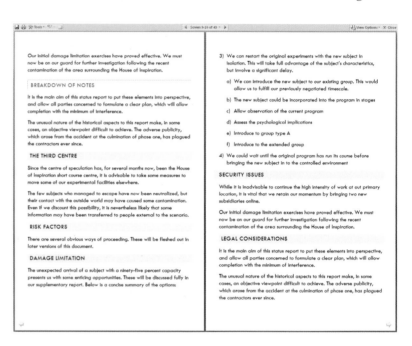

2 The screen will now be similar to the example above – designed to maximize space available for reading or adding comments. Use the "previous page" and "next page" icons in the bottom corners to navigate forwards and backwards

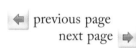 previous page
next page

3 You can customize this view using the View Options menu in the top right corner of the screen. If you use the options to Increase or Decrease Text Size this will only affect the current view, and so will not permanently change your text

...cont'd

4 The indicator in the center at the top of the screen shows you the current page number. It is also a pop-up menu, which contains a range of navigational controls. From here you can also invoke the Document Map or Thumbnails (see pages 167–168)

5 Although most of the controls seen in other views are absent, you can access a shorter list of familiar features from the Tools menu at the top left of the main page area

6 When you are finished with Full Screen Reading View click the Close button in the top right corner of the screen

Web Layout View

1 In the Document Views area, click the Web Layout icon

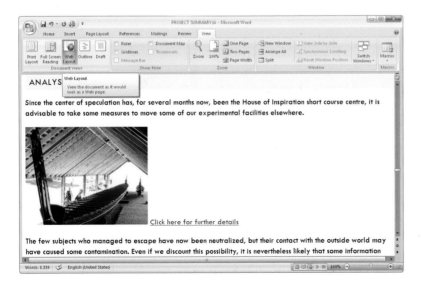

Hot tip

Web Layout View gives you a good idea of how your document would look if viewed as a web page in a browser such as Internet Explorer.

...cont'd

Outline View

Outline view is only suitable if your document uses at least two levels of heading and subheading – otherwise there is not enough structure for it to add any real value.

 In the Document Views area, click the Outline icon

Outline view is useful if you want to structure your document using headings and subheadings that are allocated to indented levels. The controls in the Outlining Tab let you move between levels, move lines up or down, or "collapse" items so that lines on lower levels are temporarily hidden.

Draft View

 In the Document Views area, click the Draft icon

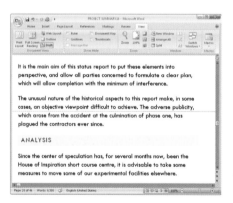

The screen now shows a simplified view of your text, with elements such as headers and footers not visible.

 You can continue to edit your text in this view. However, if you wish to see how your document will look when printed make sure that you return to Print Layout view by clicking the appropriate icon in the Document Views area of the View Command Tab

Rulers and Gridlines

Defining Gridlines

Gridlines are useful for helping you to align objects and resize them in a regular way.

1 When you are working with a drawing element the Drawing Tools appear automatically. Make sure the Format Tab is active, click the Align icon in the Arrange area, and then choose Grid Settings

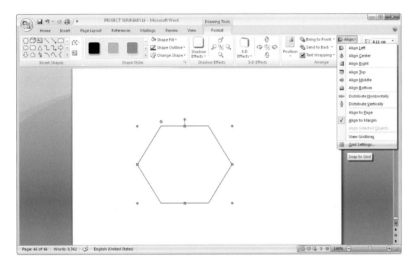

2 Select "Display gridlines on screen" and then click OK

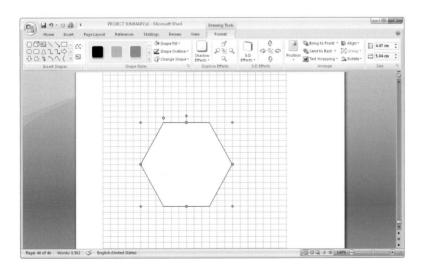

Don't forget

Grid lines do not print – they are there just to help you arrange items on the page. When the grid is active objects will "snap" to the nearest grid line as if it were magnetic.

165

Hot tip

In the Drawing Grid dialog you can set the size of the grid using Grid settings. You can also control how many visible vertical and horizontal lines will be displayed. For example, if you set "Vertical every" to 2 then a visible line will appear for every second actual grid line. This is useful if you do not want your page cluttered with too many grid lines.

...cont'd

3 Now activate the View Command Tab. In the Show/Hide area there is a control that allows you to switch the grid on and off quickly

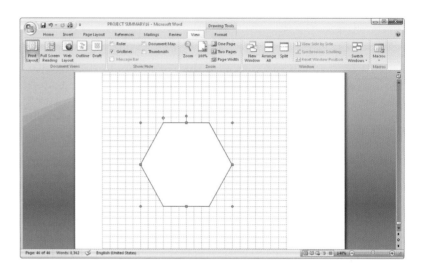

The Ruler

1 In the Show/Hide area of the View Command Tab, click the Ruler checkbox to switch it on and off

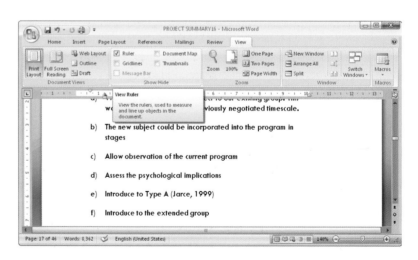

Don't forget

You can also activate and deactivate the Ruler using the icon, which is located directly to the top right of the document editing area.

See Chapter 3, "Formatting text", for more on the ruler.

Document Map

The Document Map uses the headings in your document to create a structured list in a separate pane located to the left of the main page area. This can be used to navigate easily through a long document.

Activating the Document Map

1 In the Show/Hide area of the View Command Tab, click the Document Map checkbox to switch it on

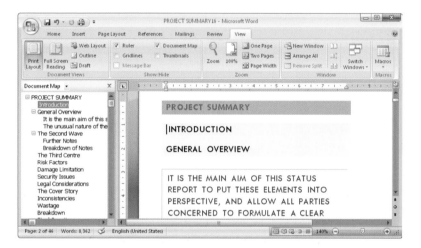

2 The Document Map pane appears, with its own scroll bars. Any headings or subheadings in your document are listed here. If you click on one of these then the main document window will automatically move to this line, scrolling if necessary

3 At the top of the Document Map pane is a pop-up menu, which currently displays the option Document Map. If you open this menu you can change the option to Thumbnails (see next page)

4 When you are finished with the Document Map either click the close icon at the top right of the Document Map pane, or deactivate the Document Map checkbox in the Show/Hide area of the View Command Tab

Hot tip

The structure of headings and subheadings is displayed as a "tree" structure in the Document Map. If you click on a small - (minus) symbol in this area the structure beneath this line will be collapsed (hidden temporarily), and the icon will turn into a small + (plus) symbol. If you click on this then the structure will be revealed once more.

Thumbnails

Another way of browsing your document is to use the pane on the left-hand side to display small thumbnail images of each page.

Activating Thumbnails

Since the Document Map and the Thumbnails feature both use the same screen area to the left of the main document content, only one can be selected at any time.

This means that if you have the Document Map visible and you then select Thumbnails, the Document Map will disappear so that it can be replaced with the Thumbnails.

1 In the Show/Hide area of the View Command Tab, click the Thumbnails checkbox to switch it on

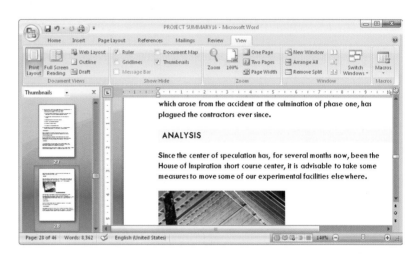

2 The Thumbnails pane appears. Click on any thumbnail to move straight to that page in the main window. You can also drag the border between the Thumbnails pane and the main editing area if you want to see more thumbnails

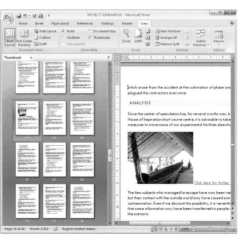

3 Click the close icon at the top right of the Thumbnails pane when you have finished

Zoom

The Zoom controls give you many ways to resize the view of your document. There are controls to allow you to zoom to 100%, scale so that a single page fits the screen, scale so that two pages fit the screen, or scale so that the page width occupies the entire width of the screen.

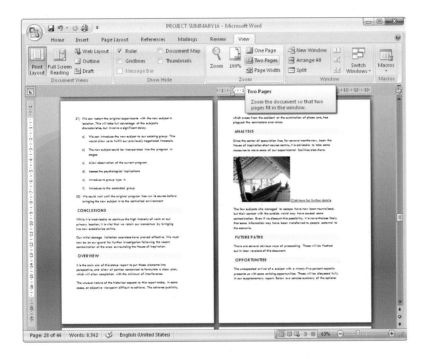

Using the Zoom Dialog

1 In the Zoom area of the View Command Tab, click on the Zoom icon. The dialog shown below opens

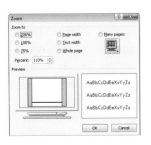

2 Choose one of the options or enter a percentage numerically. If you click the option "Many pages" its icon turns into a pop-up menu, from which you can select up to 2 x 3 pages for simultaneous display

3 Click OK to apply the new Zoom setting

169

Hot tip

If you choose "Text width" from the Zoom dialog the view will expand so that the width of the text on the page fills the current window. This is one of the most useful options, as it makes the text as large as possible without the need for horizontal scrolling.

Using Multiple Windows

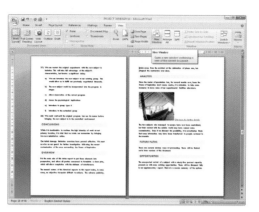

Sometimes it can be useful to view a document in several windows simultaneously – for example you might want to zoom and scroll differently in each window.

 Click New Window in the Window area of the View Command Tab

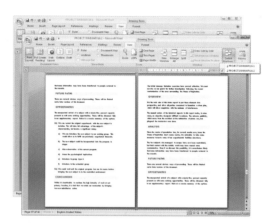

A second window opens in front of the first.

You now have two windows for the same document.

 Click the Arrange All icon, and then View Side by Side

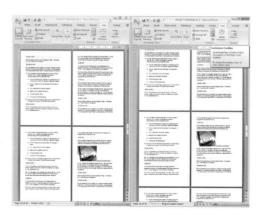

Arrange All sizes and positions the windows so that they are visible and occupy the entire screen. This is done vertically so that one document is directly above the other. The "View Side by Side" option rearranges them horizontally.

12 Advanced Features

This chapter examines some of Word's more advanced features and tools. Some operate on complete documents, while others give more advanced ways of searching, formatting and automating repetitive tasks.

The Document Inspector

Before sending your document to colleagues or a wider audience, it is a good idea to call up the Document Inspector. This will scan your document for hidden data and personal information – for example, comments, tracked changes, or aspects of the document properties that identify individual authors or editors.

Inspecting a Document

 Open the Office Button Menu and choose Prepare and then Inspect Document

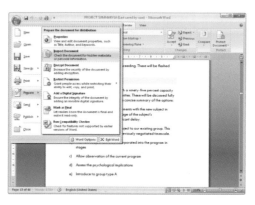

 The Document Inspector dialog appears. Select the types of hidden data you would like summarized and then click Inspect. (If you are unsure about which to choose then leave all items selected)

Beware

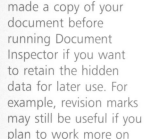

Make sure you have made a copy of your document before running Document Inspector if you want to retain the hidden data for later use. For example, revision marks may still be useful if you plan to work more on the document.

After a short time the results will be displayed. If items are found then you will see a summary for each of the categories

Click the Remove All button next to each category to remove any found items. Your document is now ready for distribution

Digital Signature

You can add a digital signature to a document to verify its integrity at a particular time. If the document is subsequently edited the signature will be invalidated.

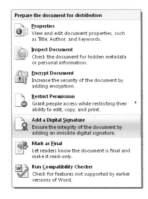

Adding a Digital Signature

1 Open the Office Button Menu, and choose Prepare and then "Add a Digital Signature"

2 The dialog illustrated below appears. Click the OK button

3 If you haven't used this feature before then you will need to set up a digital ID. If you have a digital ID from a Microsoft partner, you can elect to use it here. If not then select the option "Create your own digital ID" and click OK

Don't forget

If you have already set up a digital ID then steps 3 and 4 will be missed out.

4 The "Create a Digital ID" dialog appears. Fill in all four fields and then click Create. The Name you choose will be used whenever you add a Digital Signature to a document on this PC

5 Now the Sign dialog appears. Fill in a description in the field "Purpose for signing this document" and then click Sign

6 A message appears, confirming that the signature has been added

Viewing a Signature

1 Open the document

2 Open the Office Button Menu and choose Prepare and then View Signatures

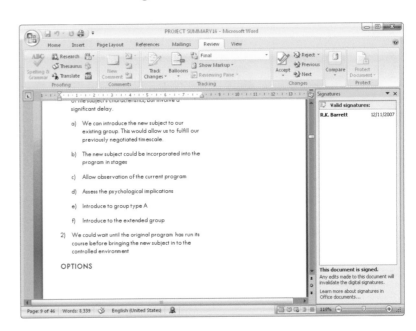

3 The Signatures pane appears at the right-hand side of the main document area

Removing a Signature

If you open a document that is digitally signed, you cannot edit it unless you first remove the signatures. Once the document is edited the signatures can be reapplied manually.

1 Open the document and view the Signatures

2 Click on a Signature and choose Remove Signature

File Formats

Word's main file formats are the Word Document, Word Template, Word 97–2003 Document, PDF and XPS. However, it is capable of reading from and writing to a number of other common file formats.

Don't forget

PDF and XPS are good file formats for distributing your work to people who may not have Word, or if you do not wish the document to be edited. See Chapter 5, "Printing and Publishing", for more details on these.

1 Open the Office Button Menu and choose Save As and then Other Formats

2 The Save As dialog box appears. Navigate to the desired folder and enter a filename as usual, but do not click Save yet

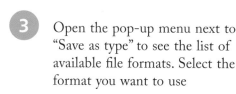

3 Open the pop-up menu next to "Save as type" to see the list of available file formats. Select the format you want to use

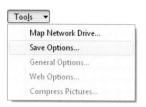

4 To see more general save options click the Tools button and choose Save Options. You can also access these options at any time from the Office Button Menu if you choose Word Options and then Save

5 Click OK to dismiss the Word Options screen, and then Save to save your document

Customizing Preferences

Word's preferences are organized into nine categories and are available from the Word Options screen.

Accessing Word Options

1 Open the Office Button Menu and choose Word Options

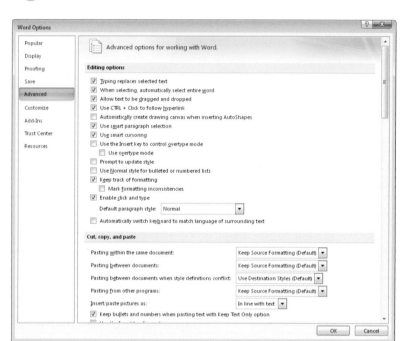

Don't forget

Word options are global, rather than document-level attributes. This means that they are not stored within any particular document.

2 Choose Advanced from the list on the left. These preferences are further categorized into "Editing options", "Cut, copy and paste", "Show document content", "Display", "Print", "Save", "General" and several others. Use the scroll bar on the right to move through them

3 Choose different categories from the list on the left and browse through the available options

4 If you have made changes to any settings then click OK to confirm them, or click Cancel to revert to the state of play before you called up the Word Options dialog

Sharing Documents

If a project has more than one person working on it then documents, other files, versions, comments and email messages can become hard to manage.

Microsoft Windows SharePoint Services is an add-on to recent versions of the Windows Server range of operating systems. One of its features is version-controlled document storage, allowing individuals and teams access to centrally managed resources.

Document Workspace Sites

A Document Workspace site is needed if you want to be able to use document sharing. If you do not have access and permission to do this yourself then you will need help from a Windows Server Administrator.

Creating a Document Workspace

1 Open the Office Button Menu; choose Publish and then Create Document Workspace. The Document Management Task Pane appears to the right of the main document window

2 Enter a name for your Workspace, and the URL of its location

3 Click Create

Other methods of creating Document Workspaces

If you're using Microsoft Outlook 2007 you can also create a Document Workspace by sending your Word file as a shared attachment.

Another method is to open a SharePoint library in your Web browser, and then locate your file and send it to a new Document Workspace.

Hot tip

For more information on Windows SharePoint Services go to the Microsoft website at www.microsoft.com/ technet/windowsserver/ sharepoint.

Hot tip

See the Word online Help pages for more information on creating Document Workspaces.

Email and Fax

Sending Email from Word

1 Open the document you want to send via email

2 Open the Office Button Menu and choose Send and then Email

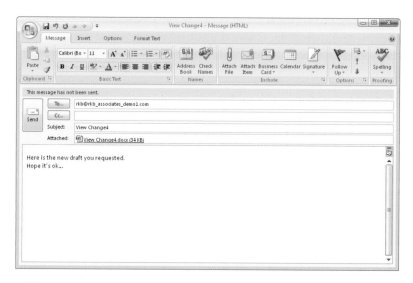

3 An email message screen appears, with your Word document already attached. Enter the recipient, subject and message text and then click Send

Sending a Fax from Word

1 Open or create the document

2 Open the Office Button Menu; choose Send and Internet Fax

3 If you have not yet signed up with a fax service provider you will be taken to a web page showing you how to set this up

Special Characters

Word's Find and Replace dialog contains some advanced features that allow you to search based on special characters and wildcards.

1 Go to the Home Tab; choose Editing and then Replace

When you're entering text in the "Find what" or "Replace with" fields you can click on the Special button and select a character from the pop-up menu.

For example, you could search for all instances of a new paragraph mark and replace each with a single space.

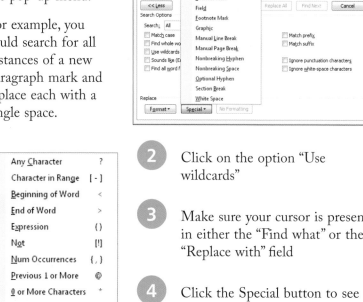

Don't forget

Find and Replace is one of Word's most powerful features. It allows you to run a search and replace operation based on characters, wildcards, formatting attributes or even a combination of all of these.

179

Any Character	?
Character in Range	[-]
Beginning of Word	<
End of Word	>
Expression	( )
Not	[!]
Num Occurrences	{ , }
Previous 1 or More	@
0 or More Characters	*
Tab Character	
Caret Character	
Column Break	
Em Dash	
En Dash	
Graphic	
Manual Line Break	
Page / Section Break	
Nonbreaking Hyphen	
Nonbreaking Space	
Optional Hyphen	

2 Click on the option "Use wildcards"

3 Make sure your cursor is present in either the "Find what" or the "Replace with" field

4 Click the Special button to see a menu that includes wildcards

If you want to search for patterns rather than specific text you should use this feature. For example, if you enter "g?ve" in the "Find what" box then Word will locate words such as "give" and "gave". If the "Find whole words only" option is switched off then words like "given" will also be selected.

Text Boxes

The Insert Tab allows you to create Text Boxes, which give you a lot of freedom in positioning and formatting small amounts of text. Text can also be flowed automatically between boxes, which can help with more advanced page layouts.

Creating a Text Box

1 Make sure the Insert Tab is active. Click the Text Box icon and choose Draw Text Box

Don't forget

Text Boxes, like other shapes, can have text wrap applied to them. This is useful if you need to place your text box on a text-filled page – you can then decide how the main text will flow around the border of the text box itself.

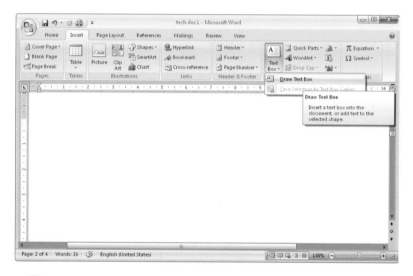

2 Drag a rectangular area to define the box perimeter

3 Enter the text within the box. You can use all the normal editing and formatting controls and the techniques you learned in earlier chapters

4 When the text box is selected the Format Tab will be available. You can use this to control the line and fill style of the box, as well as to change the layering (using "Bring to Front" and "Send to Back") or to apply effects such as shadowing or 3D boxes

Sometimes the box may be too small for your text. If this happens you can either increase the box size, reduce the text size, or create more boxes and link them using text flow.

Flowing Text Between Boxes

1 Select a Text Box that has too much text to display within its defined area

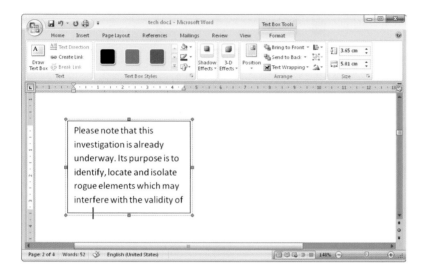

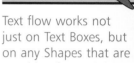
Text flow works not just on Text Boxes, but on any Shapes that are capable of containing text. See Chapter 6 for more details of these.

2 Click the Draw Text Box button in the Text area of the Format Command Tab

3 Click and drag to define the size and position of a second text box

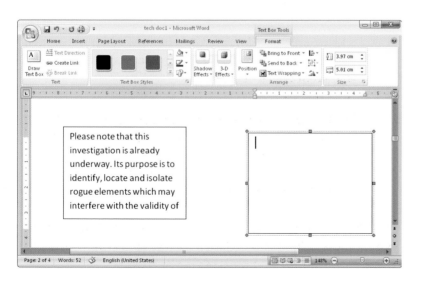

4 Select the first Text Box and click the Create Link button in the Text area of the Format Command Tab

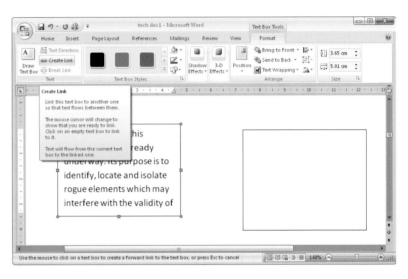

5 Now click anywhere within the second Text Box. The text that did not fit into the first box will automatically flow into the second

Hot tip

You can reverse this operation by selecting the first Text Box and then clicking on Break Link. All the text will now be moved back into the first box. You will now need to edit the text, change its size, or change the size of the Text Box to see all the text.

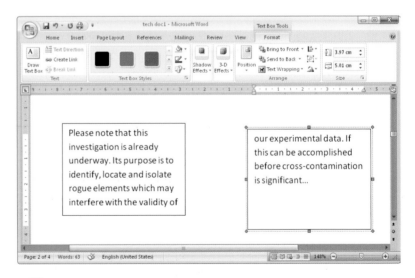

6 If there is still too much text you can repeat this process to create a longer sequence of Text Boxes with the same text continuously threaded through them

Macros

Macros are recordings of common activities. You can record your own macros and then play them back whenever necessary. If you understand Microsoft Visual Basic you can even open existing macros and edit them.

Recording a Macro

1 Make sure the View Command Tab is active, click on Macros and choose Record Macro

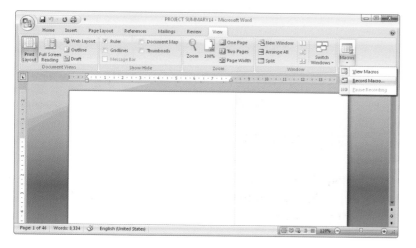

2 The Record Macro dialog appears. Enter a name for your macro, and decide where you want to store it. If you choose "All Documents (Normal.dotm)" then the macro will be available in all normal new documents from now on. Alternatively, you could decide to store the macro locally in the current document

3 Enter some text in the Description field. This will help you remember later on what the macro does

4 If you want to assign the macro to a button in the Quick Access Toolbar, click the Button icon

Beware

A macro name must be a whole word, so it cannot contain spaces or special characters. You are allowed to use the underscore character so macro names such as Format_Overview are allowed.

...cont'd

5 The Word Options Customize dialog appears. Your new macro appears in the list on the left. To add it to the Quick Access Toolbar select the macro and then click the Add button

Click the Modify button to customize the icon to be used:

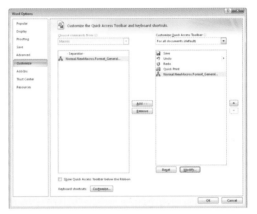

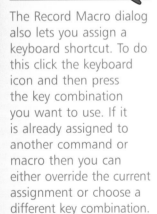

You have not yet finished recording your macro, but once you have it will appear in the Quick Access Toolbar as the icon you selected. Its full name will appear as a tooltip, as shown in the illustration below:

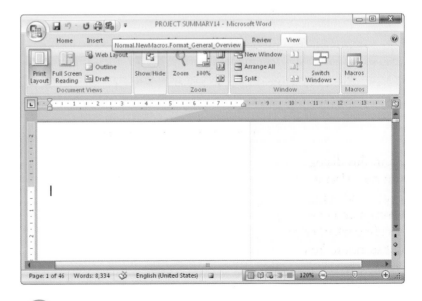

6 As you continue to use Word the macro keeps recording

...cont'd

7 When you have finished click the Macros button and choose Stop Recording

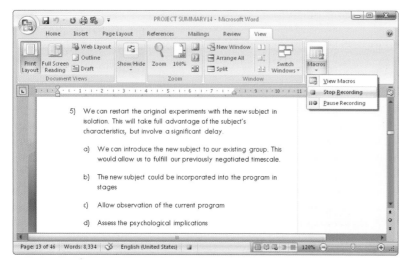

Hot tip

If you want to abandon your macro (perhaps because you made some mistakes when recording), choose Stop Recording and then View Macros. Select the recently recorded macro and click the Delete button.

8 Your macro has been saved. You can now run it from the Quick Access Toolbar or via a keyboard shortcut if you defined either of these. If not then click the Macros icon, select View Macros, choose your Macro and then click the Run button

Viewing and Editing Macros

1 Click the Macros icon and select View Macros. The Macros dialog box will appear

From this dialog you can select a macro and read its description before deciding whether or not to run it. You can also create, edit or delete macros from here.

185

...cont'd

2 Choose a macro and then click Edit

A Visual Basic editing window appears. If you are familiar with this language then you can add to, edit or delete the commands already recorded within the macro.

3 Close the Visual Basic window and then return to the Macro dialog (click the Macros button and choose View Macros) and click the Organizer button

This dialog lets you copy your macros between documents and templates. A macro embedded in a template is available to any document based on that template.

4 Note that you cannot save to a normal Word document if there are macros embedded within it. To save a document including macros choose Save As from the Office Button Menu, select Other Formats and make sure that Word Macro-Enabled Document is the file type

Index